SECRET ~~MESSAGES~~

AN

An Investigation into the Subliminal Messages

in Junior Fiction

from a Christian Perspective.

CONTENTS   Page

Chapter 1: <u>UNTANGLING THE MESSAGES</u>

"...for it is light that makes everything visible..."   (Ephesians 5:13-14)

Have you any idea what youngsters are reading today?

Parents! What are *your* children currently consuming through the written word?

Teachers! Librarians! Are you fully aware of the *contents* of the books in your libraries?

Authors! Publishers and booksellers! Do you realise that you are shaping the minds of this new generation who, as future citizens, even leaders of the nations, have the potential to influence the world?

We live in an age of fastidiousness. We employ scientists to monitor standards of hygiene and control the chemicals which invade our environment. We worry about the effects of pollution which at this moment may be poisoning us and our children. When the horse meat scare hit the headlines, it had a radical effect on the eating habits of a whole nation. Health and safety rules are paramount for every aspect of modern living, but are we as careful about purity of mind and spirit?

Whilst responsible adults are pre-occupied with the more obviously damaging influences of the internet, television and computer games, not to mention drugs and alcohol, our children are being fed insidiously through the books they read with deceptive messages which are equally as harmful as germs and chemicals. These alternative pollutants are being distributed legally every day under the cover of children's fiction, available in high-street chain-stores and on-line, in public libraries and on school bookshelves.

Reading is a socially acceptable and educational pastime. Compared with other more recognisable dangers, children's books are considered quite innocuous, thus allowing their secret messages to slip through unnoticed by all but the most discerning. One might even assume that the modern child is too busy to read! On the contrary, the Common Sense Media Survey of 2013 found that children still read books for half an hour per day on average, in spite of the increased use of screens large and small. A spokesman for Walker Books says, "The profile of children's books has never been higher". In fact, sales of junior fiction across all formats rose to £349 million in 2014, a rise of 11% on the previous year. Exports of UK published children's books rose by 28% in that year. According to John Dougherty, author of *Stink Bomb and Ketchup Face*, publishers are more prepared to "take a punt" on edgier, riskier works in this genre.

The Power of the Word

Consider the power of the word, written or spoken. If sharp words have been exchanged, the atmosphere in the room seems highly inflammable. A sarcastic or hurtful remark will ring in your ears for a long time. Yet words may be used to encourage the downhearted or calm the panic-stricken. They may be used to edify or degrade both speaker and receiver. The Bible tells us that God used words to create the universe!

St. Matthew said, "Out of the overflow of the heart the mouth speaks" (Mat.12:34). It follows then that the words received by a reader have come from the heart of the writer. Authors come from the whole spectrum of humanity, from every faith or no faith; those with a vision, who pass on their own experience of blessing and understanding, or those with an axe to grind or a warped set of values. They use their medium to make statements reflecting their own ideas and philosophies as any creative artist would. Their messages, though hidden behind a façade of exciting imagery, are deep and powerful.

Fertile Ground

All readers are vulnerable to the persuasions of the written word, but *children* are especially to be protected since their analytical ability is still undeveloped. They trust what they read; they want to believe what adults tell them. The young reader has not yet learned to be cynical or sophisticated. These attitudes are caught from adults, sooner or later, as part of the growing up process.

To children, life is simple, straight-forward and immensely interesting. Their curiosity drives them on with ever deepening questions about the world around them, about life, about truth. They want to know "Who am I?" and "How do I fit into the total picture?" They also need security and to know the boundaries of what is right and acceptable.

Children know, indeed they are taught at school, that a book is a good place to find something out, and whether they realise it or not, they are finding answers to their questions in everything they read. Grahame Green said, "Perhaps it is only in childhood that books make a deep impression on us". The image and imagery of printed words impress themselves on children's minds, instilling attitudes and values, offering models and goals, giving spiritual and moral insights of all kinds.

The very way in which the reading activity takes place – quietly, comfortably, maybe curled up on a cushion, unhurried, undisturbed – increases the ability to absorb these concepts deeply, even subconsciously, like subliminal messages. Our earliest experience of books is of being cuddled by mum as she reads an exciting and coherent text (so different from ordinary conversation), or interprets colourful and lively pictures. We may also associate this activity with bed-time stories from dad, who is usually so busy, but earmarks this time to ensure contact with his child. It is an activity full of reassurance and security. For others, for whom this setting is unrealistic, books become a means of escape from friction, noise or trauma – a safe refuge.

As children begin to read for pleasure, and not solely to satisfy the teacher, they become increasingly proficient at registering the events of a story by means of mental pictures in order to assimilate their meaning. The eye often backtracks, so that a line or a theme may be re-read several times for full comprehension. Thus the significance of the text may be taken in more deeply than when merely listening to a story, or watching a film, which moves on at a faster pace.

Children's minds, then, are fertile ground. Young readers are willing to learn through the attractive medium of modern publishing. So, what seeds are being planted? May we assume junior fiction comprises an infinite variety of wholesome tales written in Standard English?

Unfortunately the answer is, "No". In recent decades the literary climate has definitely changed. Once, children's books were a tool for imparting Christian values and upholding our cultural identity. Then came the liberal society and a rejection of convention. Though much of children's publishing is now superior in the quality of presentation, its content is far from predictable and may hold some nasty surprises. Tattered copies of traditional stories, even modern classics and favourites from the fifties, have been cleared from libraries to make way for contemporary stock.

Responsibility

Very often, parents leave their offspring to make their own judgements and decisions, though many would actually prefer guidance. It would seem that though Britain's youngsters are now materially well-off, they are morally and spiritually deprived. Their knowledge of the historic religious faith of this country, the faith which has inspired many of its greatest men and women, is now very sadly lacking.

It would be a mistake to leave parental responsibility for children's reading in the hands of librarians, whose criteria for selection are open to question. According to one county librarian, the prime consideration in selecting a new book is its appeal to children, closely followed by readability and subject interest. In *Buying Books* (*1) Ann Parker states "Subject matter should have the potential to widen the reader's sympathy and understanding and extend imagination". I would question how far a child is expected to sympathise with and understand those whose philosophies are undesirable. There must be limits. She argues that the viewpoint must be genuine and convincing. Well, an author who is a convinced anarchist may indeed be genuine!

For teachers, who have great responsibility towards their pupils, it is becoming increasingly necessary to "vet" books used in school to avoid embarrassment or regret for harm done. Some novels used as class-readers have caused both parents and pupils some anxiety. So our concern is not only about books that children may choose for themselves, but also those which they are obliged to read or listen to and discuss.

In this category we find set-books and, at the lower levels, school reading schemes. Though in the past the rather bland Peter and Jane series (Ladybird books) achieved their aim, to teach children to read by means of graded vocabulary and repetition, nevertheless they were reckoned insufficiently exciting by today's standards. Many newer sets of "readers" use lively humour and colourful pictures, but include violent and occult themes too.

It is misguided to feed this craving for action with examples of breaking the rules of acceptable behaviour, when there are so many legitimate ways of achieving this end. A story may be exciting because it embodies something that the child would love to be able to do if only his own limitations would allow. To read about a child who succeeds in skating or horse-riding say, or overcomes a challenge, can be a means of sharing an uplifting experience of achievement otherwise unattainable. Infants especially need wholesome food and tender care so that they may grow both in the mechanics of reading and in their experience of those aspects of life which are noble, pure and lovely (Phil.4:8). There lies the essence of true excitement and inspiration.

Surely these goals are desirable for all ages. It would seem that what is bad for children is probably equally unedifying for adults too, though the latter are better able to cope with its influence. So in setting a pattern for children, perhaps we may establish a standard which will not be abandoned in adulthood.

<u>The Purpose of the Book</u>

Stories fall into many categories: mysteries, adventures, historical novels, science-fiction and a vast range of fantasy literature. I intend to take more general themes in the first part of this book, looking at how writers deal with subjects like spirituality, personal relationships and violence. Finally I shall discuss the treatment of more specific types of book such as fantasy, the occult and humour. The works of popular writers may contain a full blend of the elements investigated, from the supernatural and violence through to propaganda and attitudes to authority. Authors are in the business of delivering messages!

With an estimated 10,000 books published for children every year, my survey can by no means be exhaustive. Space does not allow adequate coverage of poetry, comics, magazines or text-books, though occasional reference to these is made to illustrate a trend. However, I hope I have covered a fair sample, sufficient to offer as a guide. My research has concentrated on material for the 3-13 year-olds. Occasionally I have referred to a title in the teenage range in order to pursue a theme.

My purpose in writing this book is not to pronounce judgements on certain blacklisted titles. Rather, I hope to alert and challenge the discerning adult, by means of a series of questions that you might ask yourself regarding the kinds of books you would be happy for your children to read. What messages would you want them to receive? I hope that you will use these questions as a checklist for guidance as you buy or borrow, with or for children, so that we may all become more aware of the dangers.

It is encouraging that a growing number of parents and teachers are concerned about this problem, but many are still unsure how to express exactly what is wrong. I hope to clarify the issues. Many people, even if not professing a religion, would still hold a moral viewpoint based on the laws and conventions of this nation which have arisen out of the Christian tradition. I therefore suggest that standards are measured against those laid down by the Author of the greatest life-giving book, the Bible, whose teachings have stood the test of time and still stand today. Children approach life with a questioning mind, searching for truth and fairness. We are letting the younger generation down if we allow lowered standards to go unchallenged.

On Radio 4's Museum of Curiosities programme recently, the presenters were discussing children's literature. They confidently agreed that it doesn't matter what you read as long as you read it! Comments like this only serve to highlight the widespread ignorance of the problem. Children do not have perfect discernment, nor is it true that any book that is attractive, even well-written, must be good. Another of the panel asked, "What is wrong with low-quality fiction?" I hope this book will provide some answers.

Footnote *1:   Published by Youth Libraries Group of the Library association

Chapter 2:   THE CHRISTIAN ETHOS

"… Find out what pleases the Lord…"   (Eph.5:10)

A) Does the book comply or conflict with the Christian ethos?

1) Is God *present*, or at least, is there room for him?

Considering the fact that nowadays the majority of people in the UK would not adhere to any particular faith, it is surprising how frequently religious themes and terminology are used in modern junior fiction. Therefore to avoid confusion, for the purposes of *this* investigation "God" refers to the God of the Bible, who named himself the Lord Almighty. He came in the flesh as Jesus Christ to die as our saviour and came alive again as victor over death and evil. Therefore his power is greater than any other.

As we shall see, in fiction other powers (gods with a small "g") may rule over a scenario and command obeisance. These gods, or God, may form an integral part of the story, be present by implication, or be ignored completely.

1.1) There may be a god present, but which one?

Back in 1956 when Ian Serraillier wrote *The Silver Sword*, we knew exactly to which god Ruth was responding when she exclaimed, "Thank God, they're safe", since her own courage and selfless attitude had been inspired by the Bible stories she had taught in her make-shift school.

More recently, Tanith Lee's *The Winter Players* is brazenly religious. Oaive is the priestess, the lady of the shrine. She makes offerings at an altar, officiates at the sunset ritual and guards the special relics which are "the source of the shrine's holiness". The mysterious Grey comes to her for absolution and blessing. Who is *their* god?

However, in Judy Blume's *Are You There, God? It's Me Margaret,* although the name of the heroine's God is in no doubt, since he is claimed by both the Christian and the Jewish wings of the family, one only has to read the first chapter to realise that this is not everyone's idea of a "Christian" book. The reference to smelly armpits on the first page is a signal to the reader that the author has no respect for taboo subjects and is definitely out to shock.

Margaret is continually praying, indeed, elects to make a study of religion as her special project at school. However, for all this, she never receives any response from God. She visits a church and a synagogue in order to compare the two, but to her disappointment, the special feeling of God's presence that she longs to find is absent from both. The message is: God is abstract, indifferent, holding us at arm's length. This is obviously not God the Father that Jesus believed in!

So, whilst Jehovah may be present, the author might even through ignorance have given him attributes contrary to Bible teaching, thus taking on the role of false prophet. We must not only ask, "Which god is present?" but, if it is the Christian God then, "Is his character portrayed truthfully as revealed in the Bible?"

1.2) If God is present, is his portrayal Biblically accurate?

Patricia St.John makes it very clear in all her novels that God is sovereign. In *Nothing Else Matters*, Amin, who is an adolescent in troubled Lebanon, is searching for a meaning to life: "Somewhere there must be a God who is alive …. a Creator …Someone who controls the stars and the sea and makes things grow?" An open questioning attitude is healthy and to be expected as children grow up. Our God is big enough to withstand challenges. Jesus who is The Truth and The Way (Jn.14:6) said, "Seek and you will find" (Lk.11:9).

Amin teases his Maronite mother when she prays before a crucifix, but he asks a serious question, "Can a dead Christ help us? The reader does not have long to wait before the answers begin to flow. It is evident from this story that God permeates the whole of life even when not specifically mentioned. Amin's sister Lamia turns to the Bible where she finds comfort and feels "her broken heart warmed". This is a sincere attempt to portray what Christianity is really about.

However, in Ted Hughes' *Tales of the Early World*, we see a drastic distortion of God's character and a denial of his supremacy as Creator and Source of Life. Contrary to Genesis 1:31 where God surveyed all he had made and saw "it was very good", the god of Hughes' imagination is seen as a bungler who makes mistakes and whose creation is not therefore perfect. Neither is he all powerful nor omniscient. In fact he often appears perplexed, and under the thumb of his mother!

Consider the implications! She is depicted as a wizened old creature, an older power than God, whose magic is able to produce a baby for Eve, thus bringing her life that God was unable to induce! She also creates a tiger as a protector for the child. "God was mystified. This was the first he'd ever heard of angels". The cover blurb dares to claim that this is one of the Poet Laureate's finest works!

The portrayal of God may sometimes quite legitimately be veiled by allegory. The classic example is found in the *Chronicles of Narnia* by C.S. Lewis where we glimpse the person of Jesus through Aslan, the Mighty Lion. His character is admirably assessed by Mr Beaver (*The Lion, the Witch and the Wardrobe*) when Lucy asks if Aslan is safe. He exclaims, "Whatever gave you that idea? He's not safe! He's wild. But very, very good". The reader is filled with reverential awe for this powerful beast and at the same time is given spiritual insight regarding the concept of Godly fear.

Similarly we sense the trepidation of Fay Sampson's little cat, Pangur Ban (*Pangur Ban the White Cat*) as he is gently carried in Arthmael's mouth. This great dolphin, portrayed as the "clown of God", epitomizes the joy of life. Though misunderstood and wounded, his blood saves the princess from death. Through fantasy we see the grace of God for the undeserving, and resurrection for the saviour.

1.3) Is Scripture quoted, or paraphrased, accurately and in context?

Whilst it is important to check that Bible stories are reproduced faithfully according to the truth as we have received it, those written for children are usually paraphrased from the original for easy reading and to avoid unsuitable themes. There is no mention of Rahab being a prostitute in Dave Hill's *The Walls Come Tumbling Down*, (one of the excellent Arch Book series) which retells the battle of Jericho in verse. This is an acceptable selection of detail without detracting from the main event.

Peter Dickinson's imaginative retelling of thirty-three Old Testament stories in *City of Gold* forces the important issue: How much may we change the word of God? (Rev.22:18-19). In his first story, *The Fall of Man*, Eve asks Adam why she must not eat of the fruit of the Tree of Knowledge. Adam replies that he does not know, even though in the Bible version God clearly warns of resulting death. Dickinson states that before Eve appeared, the serpent had been a close companion of Adam, "sitting under the stars together and riddling out the wonders of God's creation". He suggests that the serpent was jealous of Eve.

This fanciful translation must of course be weighed against the author's accurate portrayal of the one powerful yet merciful God, and the honesty of his notes at the back of the book regarding his philosophy. He views these stories as legends which have grown to suit the times and makes no apology for amalgamating some of the details. However, the distorting of the word of God is just what the serpent did in Genesis 3 and so cannot be right.

In Madeleine L'Engle's *A Wrinkle in Time*, the three Beasts of Uriel partially quote Romans 8:28 & 30: "We are called according to his purpose and whom he calls, them he also justifies". These words actually refer to people who have been justified by faith in Jesus, but the verse which mentions his name has been omitted. The passage in Romans speaks of God's love and protection, but when Meg, the heroine, asks who helps her to fight evil, there is no reference to God or even the angels which figure prominently in the story. The Beasts say," Good helps us … the stars …light …love. In a book laced with religious language it seems odd to ignore God at this point.

If a writer quotes Scriptures but omits the Bible references, this makes it difficult to check its accuracy, which is sometimes found wanting. Be on guard against Scripture quoted out of context in order to support the author's own persuasions. Anyone can find a Biblical passage to prove a point, but to really hear what God is saying the Bible message needs to be taken as a whole.

A2) Is the scenario one that excludes God? If so, how?

Even though God may not be mentioned explicitly in a story, his presence might be implied by reference to church halls, vicars, Easter eggs, Christmas, or even the use of his name as an expletive! At a deeper level, when moral motives and values are upheld, one is aware of a spiritual depth in the widest sense which goes beyond humanism and materialism. So we ask, "Is there room for God? Is there a place for him in this created scenario?" A negative answer would pose further questions.

There are various reasons why there might be no place for God. Perhaps the alternative god is the reader himself. "You are the ultimate referee whose word is law" states the cover blurb of *Monster Horrorshow* by J.H. Brennan. This is typical of many role-playing books where the reader decides which course the story will take.

God would obviously be excluded if other deities were central to the story. In this multi-cultural climate libraries are stocking literature from many other faiths. You may feel that it benefits a child's general knowledge to be exposed to the legends from around the world, and even to the basics of the major religions. However, one would do well to ask, "How are the stories being presented?" If they are being offered as undisputed truth, then reading more than one could be very confusing, especially for immature readers.

Exclamations invoking the name of Allah are frequently used by the fictional characters of Islamic stories and are of course simultaneously reiterated by the reader. In Ruskin Bond's *Tales and Legends from India*, the stories reflect the worship of the sun-god and other Hindu deities such as Krishna, Durga and Shiva, the god of war and destruction with power over life and death. Sacrifice, re-incarnation and karma are all taken for granted.

Myths and legends from other cultures could perhaps be used to convey a moral truth or provide historical details of a bygone age. However, central to Susan Price's tale, *Odin's Monster,* is the Norse god of death and dangerous magic. Kveldulf Witch, who derives power from him, repays him for favours with a man's life. He uses a corpse filled with dead souls to torment the hero, Thord Cat, who is saved by Freya the fertility goddess. For a "happy" ending, Cat marries the witch queen and they produce many little witches. It is not difficult to decide how this story measures against our criteria!

It would be reasonable to suppose that Greek mythology provides plenty of material for excitement and adventure, whilst giving an insight into Greek civilisation. Perhaps *The Voyage of Odysseus*, as retold by James Reeves, might provide valuable facts about this important people who helped to shape the world. Reeves is to be commended for explaining in the prologue that in ancient Greece, everyone believed in gods who lived on Mt. Olympus, expecting prayer and sacrifice, yet possessing very human traits of greed, jealousy and strife, and given to interfering in the affairs of men. But I wonder if the young reader will remember the prologue, supposing that he did bother to read it, when he arrives at chapters 4 and 5 and is harshly informed − "The anger of the gods is swift to punish the insolence of men…"   and   "Men do not decide their own fates. They are in the hands of the immortal gods who rule the earth from their thrones on lofty Mt Olympus".

2.1) If God is not present, what values are being promoted?

When God is absent, we cannot expect Christian values to underlie the attitudes of the heroes, nor the working out of the plot. Once an alternative scenario has been set up, with other gods in control, anything might happen. There is the opportunity for an author to turn conventions upside-down, establish a new set of rules and promote his own pet philosophy. Normal reactions may be reversed. Even the meanings of words may be changed.

Odysseus is described as wise, tactful, resourceful and courageous in battle. On returning from Troy, he is forced to land at Ismarus where he lays waste the city and plunders the whole country in order to fill his ships with food and wine. The message given is that this is a wise and resourceful action. The attribute of "cunning" is constantly used as though synonymous with "clever", yet today the word is defined as "selfish cleverness or skill in deceit" (Oxford Dictionary). From the narrative, this would more accurately describe the hero's actions. Odysseus allows his other eleven ships to sail into Laestrygonian Harbour where they are sitting targets, whilst he himself moors safely outside.

The blurb on the dust-jacket of *Master of Fiends*, by Douglas Hill, states that this "tense, enthralling fantasy adventure pulls the reader into a frighteningly barbaric and untamed world, governed by the forces of dark sorcery". Though the atmosphere throughout is essentially "spiritual", there is obviously no place for a loving God whose purpose is to defeat the power of evil.

Here the Demon-Driver is resisted by 12-year-old Jarral and his three "courageous" friends who use special powers to rescue their leader, wizard Cryltaur. Of course, in a world devoid of the power of Jesus Christ, it is not surprising that Scythe says of the evil spirits, "They know we can't really hurt them". However, Jarral does have the ability to summon fire and rain, described as nature spirits, which are able to battle against demonic attack. Christians believe that it is God the creator who has the ultimate authority over all creation.

It should not surprise us that continual violence is depicted in *Seas of Blood*, (Jackson and Livingstone) where the mountains of Enraki are the home of warrior priests, fearsome holy men armed by the gods of war and protected by gods of stone. People's lifestyles are directly related to the kind of god they acknowledge. The nature of the fictional deity will dictate the general ethos of the novel.

In *A Harp of Fishbones* by Joan Aiken, villagers come to the goddess of the mountain with precious offerings to pray for deliverance. Because they do not honour her with music, she becomes filled with irrational and vengeful anger, cursing the people with burning, then freezing. The heroine breaks the curse with her harp music, promising to play in her honour every day.

The Christian truth is that it is not by anything *we* can do, but by God's grace that we are saved from condemnation into eternal life through Jesus. The nature of God is one of justice tempered with mercy. He is always true to that nature, never irrational. Maybe it is the unpredictability of these pagan gods that gives such an aimless and oppressive atmosphere to their stories.

A typical example is *A Wizard of Earthsea* (by Ursula Le Guin), namely Ged who, forever running away from the evil spirit he has evoked, has "no clear plan … he must run …but where?" The world of Earthsea is a fantasy land where our God has no place, but witchcraft and pagan gods are taken for granted. The wizard Ogion is called "he who holds the earthquake on a leash". The reader is told that Segoy made the islands of the world, and the Terranon Stone "… knows all births and deaths and beings before and after death, the unborn and the undying, the bright world and the dark one". To quote the Times Ed, the author's beliefs "owe something to Existentialism and eastern philosophies".

A3) Does the book convey purpose in life?

3.1) Is life seen to have meaning, order and pattern?

From a very young age, children are seeking to know what makes the world tick. They soon discover what happens if ….? "If I cry loud enough I will be cuddled; if I touch the fire it will burn me; in winter I feel cold". Certain things are predictable. They follow normal patterns of behaviour and obey natural laws. There is a security in this knowledge that enables children to cope better with the extra-ordinary when it eventually happens.

The need for security in consistency and order has been initiated in us by our Creator who promised (Gen.8:22) : "As long as the earth endures, seedtime and harvest, cold and heat, summer and winter, day and night will never cease". He is a God with a purpose for his world. He is dependable, always the same, and gives meaning to life.

When other gods are supposedly in charge, there is no assurance of their good intent. Oaive (*The Winter Players*) questions, "Do you suppose God is playing with us? Some god or other?" Even the inconsistency here between God and god emphasises the unanswered question, and puts doubt in the reader's mind. In the same book, villagers give allegiance to a fickle god, lord of the fish. He sometimes sends fish aground on the beach to feed the people, but at other times does not. No reason is given; no care is shown by this god.

In a more domestic setting, the same message is being given by L'Engle's Meg in *A Wind in the Door*. After a spate of mindless vandalism and burglaries in the neighbourhood, she feels that everything is falling apart, "unsafe and precarious". She has "a cold awareness of the uncertainty of all life". Maybe adults have to face uncertainties, but surely children must learn about the certainties first?

Though Ged, the wizard of Earthsea, *appears* to have a purpose, first in fleeing the evil shadow that pursues him, and later to turn and hunt it down, nevertheless the saga is written in such a depressingly hypnotic style that we almost take it for granted that there is no joy and no enlightenment. Ged loses the shadow for a while and is shipwrecked, but the couple who take him in are scared of him. There is no happiness even in the rescue, only desolation: "Now their hut is gone and the storms of many winters have left no sign of the two who lived out their lives there and died alone". We sense that all is meaningless.

Eventually he finds himself face to face with the evil thing. "No wizardry could save him now, but only his life itself against the unliving". Why? No explanation is given about why the wizardry we have been led to believe is so amazing could not now save him! These powers then cannot be relied upon for help or direction. It is said of Ged that he had nothing to guide him "except the luck of the world's wind".

3.2) Does the book portray life as pure chance?

More discussion will be offered in later chapters regarding role-playing fantasy books, like *Seas of Blood*. However, reference must be made to them at this point because they promote the concept of life being pure chance, dependant on a snap decision or the roll of a dice. This arises from the theory that the universe has evolved by a random process and excludes the Creator's role. The plans of God for his world have been superseded by the element of luck.

When, in the final chapter of *Master of Fiends*, the heroes have saved the world, they reflect on "all the moments when success or failure, life or death, had hung like a tremulous thread – when only a small shift in their fortunes might have carried them to destruction and the world to many more long ages of monstrous rule".

If everything hangs on chance, then life *is* meaningless, but this message of hopelessness ignores the truth that Jesus came to bring life in all its fullness (John 10:10). This world has been created with infinite variety and potential, coupled with order and purpose for the future. A child's hunger for excitement *can* be satisfied from the basis of what is sure and true. If we take these things away, we deprive him of security. A world without any certainty brings a spirit of restless anxiety.

A4) What is there beyond life?

4.1) Is death portrayed as final?

When considering the purpose of life, one is immediately confronted with the challenge of death. Children's books today reflect the fact that many are sceptical about life after death. We sense this futility of life and the finality of the end in *Tipper Wood's Revenge* (by T.R. Burch) when a man is shot during a bank robbery. The officials arrive: "… Within a minute or two everything would be tidied up and cleared away. A man's life had come to an end and all that mattered was the proper disposal of the body … It had all happened before, many times … The dark pool (of blood) slithered into the gutter and disappeared...".

In *Andi's War*, by Billi Rosen, the hurt and pain of death are emphasised, but no reassurance is given. In a country where Greek Orthodoxy is the state religion, it would have been easy to bring in the hope of heaven at the time of her brother's funeral, but Andi says, "The lid was at last put over him, shutting him off from me for ever".

We must not deprive children of the good news: that Jesus offers eternal life with him, which will be far better than this. The gospel hope counteracts the fear of death, as Patricia St.John's works, especially *The Tanglewoods' Secret*, clearly illustrate.

4.2) What message is given about life after death and the spiritual realm?

Douglas Hill's view of eternity suggests universal salvation when, in *Master of Fiends*, he refers to the eternal rest of natural death, though he warns that one slain by the sorcerer's sword will become a wraith, destined to be tormented by evil spirits forever in the Farther Darkness. What injustice!

From Norse legend comes the theory, in *Odin's Monster*, that the souls of recently deceased people and animals, roaming the darkness of night, are in danger of being caught in a soul-trap hung in a tree by a witch. They will then be placed into a corpse in order to revive it and enable it to go a-haunting. When Thord Cat is tormented in this way he orders the ghostly "Sending" to kill Kveldulf Witch instead. The Queen advises Cat "When you bury Kveldulf you must drive a good thick long wooden stake through his heart, deep into the earth beneath him, to pin him to his grave. Put a large boulder on top, to make it hard for him to come out". One can hardly miss the message. Is your child scared of graveyards? Where did that fear come from?

The Bible makes it clear that heaven or paradise is not the same as the heavenly or spiritual realm (cf. Eph.6:12 and Luke 23:43). The former is the place where God dwells and is the eternal destiny of all who accept the salvation of Christ, thus rendering the fear of death unnecessary. The latter is the battle ground for opposing forces, unseen rulers and powers.

The Bible describes these spirit-beings as either angels, or demons which are fallen angels on Satan's side in rebellion against God. When people die they become neither angels nor demons. In fiction children are more likely to read about the demons and ghosts than to be reassured about the presence of angels, even though these powers for good are free to roam all realms.

Donald Bisset seems to be completely confused on this subject. In his short story for younger readers *Hotty and the Blackbird* (from *Sleep Tight Snakey Boo*) we find an angel up in the sky wondering if he is real because "angels are really imaginary things". He decides, "Yes I am! I'm an imaginary angel, and that is the best kind". To add to this confusion, the angel then has a conversation with a fairy-godmother, also confirmed as imaginary, thus placing the two in the same category. As an aside the author states, "Angels by the way are its, not hes or shes". Has he never read of Gabriel and Michael? (Daniel 8-10) Bisset's stories in the main are quite inane yet slipped amongst them we find these false messages.

False indeed is the picture given in *A Wrinkle in Time* regarding angels. Here they are manifested as elderly women, Mrs Who, Mrs Whatsit and Mrs Which, who is actually depicted as a witch: "…a figure in a black robe and black peaked hat, beady eyes, a beaked nose and long grey hair; one bony claw clutched a broomstick".

Is this just ridiculous or is it sinister?

4.3) In whose hand is the power over life and death?

In *Master of Fiends*, Gradd asserts "all beings should be able to choose the place and manner of their dying". Is this a plea for euthanasia or even suicide? *The Shadow Guests* by Joan Aiken is the story of Cosmo whose mother and brother have committed suicide in order to break an ancient curse on elder sons of the family. The impression given is that using one's own death to effect spiritual victory, though regrettable, is the only way.

Similarly, the wizard of Earthsea hopes to drown his evil pursuer and himself with it "so at least his death would put an end to the evil he had loosed by living". To bring about some good at last by dying appeals to the guilty conscience, just as dying in order to pay a penalty makes sense to the rational thinker. The truth is that taking one's own life in attempt to atone for sin is the devil's own deception and tempts man to take the place of God. No man has been good enough to pay the price of sin except Jesus Christ, and he was God.

Suicide amongst young people today is at a highly unacceptable level. Childline receives a call every half hour from youngsters considering suicide. Teenage depression has increased by 70% in the past 25 years. According to the Young Minds Organisation (2016), 1 in 4 young people in the UK have suicidal thoughts while 1 in 10 suicides are committed by 15-24 year-olds. Data from the Mental Health Foundation shows that suicide is the leading cause of death in the UK among 20-34 year-olds. One has to ask whether the new age of children's writing has contributed to these negative attitudes.

A5) How is the church portrayed?

5.1) What view is given of clergy and churches?

Fear of grave-yards inevitably leads to misconceptions of churches. Such ideas are sown by eerie stories of ghosts such as we find in *The Ghost of Thomas Kempe* by Penelope Lively. This book, a winner of the Library Association's Carnegie Medal, recounts a lengthy exorcism of the nineteenth century. Though conducted with bell, book and candle, much incantation and exhortation, the vicar "was obliged to abandon his ritual speech. It was clearly having no effect at all". He resorted to catching the spirit in a bottle and corking it up!

Bert, wart-charmer and water-diviner is portrayed as the expert and is brought in to find a solution. He insinuates that if the ghost has no respect for the church, it is a waste of time bringing in the clergy. This is a deception, for it is the name and authority of Jesus that has power over demons, according to Christian doctrine. Kempe's spirit is finally laid to rest when Bert places the pipe and spectacles of the deceased on his tomb in the vault! What superstition is this?

It is this sort of narrative that perpetuates the notion that churches are cold and fusty and all about ritual. Almost an aside, in *Cry of a Seagull*, Monica Dickens includes a cameo of an old church, gaunt and grey with its windows boarded up. "Never build that up again, they won't" is the comment. This scene of dereliction is emphasised by the presence of loiterers with "dead eyes" and an old woman looking like a jumble sale.

Though we may regret the promotion of the "dying church" image, rather than the warm and friendly one, still we have to admit the reality that some do exist. However, it would be good to see a balance maintained. Both *Me Jill Robinson and the Stepping Stones Mystery* by Anne Digby, and the delightful fantasy *A Gift From Winklesea* by Helen Cresswell mention church-going as a normal part of life, but these are in the minority. Many secular authors only seek to denigrate Christianity. The clergy are often seen as a joke, as in Westall's *The Scarecrows*.

5.2) How are Christians portrayed?

Several false ideas are sown in *Are You There, God. It's Me, Margaret*. The Christian grand-parents are depicted as the trouble-makers who break up the family and cause misery. From their mouths comes the statement, "A person doesn't choose religion … A person's born to it". In the case of Christianity, this is a complete reversal of the truth. Margaret considers that she would rather be born into it than try to choose between them, since all faiths are much the same and only cause friction! Her parents, who merely celebrate "the December traditional holiday", are portrayed as wisely avoiding controversy.

The belief that any religion is better than none is held by Laura's Gran in *The Finding* by Nina Bawden. When our heroine meets an evangelist at the fair who tells her to bring her family to the mission tent, she decides to invite her Gran who goes to church sometimes. This implies that her parents do not, and reinforces the lie that church is for the elderly and female.

At the service, a strange representation of the phenomenon of "falling in the spirit" is given: "She lay jerking and kicking on the ground, her skirt caught between her knees, showing her underwear". The preacher thunders, "Let her lie where Jesus flung her". This is a grossly exaggerated picture of indignity: ridicule arising out of ignorance. No wonder Alex is frightened and thinks it all a sham. Of course it is *his* reaction as hero that will carry weight with the readers.

One wonders at the inclusion of this incident, which has little to do with the plot. Here is a highly topical theme involving an adopted child who runs away to the city. Yet lurking between the pages are some misrepresentations of Christianity. Everyone is worried about Alex's disappearance, so Laura tries to pray like the missioners. She copies what she has seen, swaying, shouting, groaning, making herself giddy. Mr Fowles, portrayed as the "bad-guy", also promises to pray. The implication is that he is a hypocrite. What does all this suggest to readers about those who pray?

It appears that this author has a personal axe to grind against Christians, for in her earlier book, *Carrie's War*, the story of three evacuees, we find another hypocrite, Mr Samuel Isaac Evans. This character, who is "terribly chapel", is over-bearing, unjust, mean, the one we love to hate, yet supposedly is the vehicle by which the Christian viewpoint is conveyed. Perhaps Ms Bawden has something to work out of her own past as an evacuee. Has she had churchianity thrust at her? If so, much as we may sympathise, we must recognise that she is passing on those same feelings to her readers.

We even find hypocrisy rearing its head in one of Roald Dahl's "humorous" works, *The Witches*. The grandmother tells all kinds of enormous lies about witches having blue spit and wearing wigs. Then it is revealed that she goes to church every day and says grace at every meal! Are children to believe that Christians tell lies, or that these details about witches are true?

In *Andi's War*, we find Marco actually accusing Jesus of being a hypocrite and a communist. Christianity is portrayed as being oppressive when he is forced to take communion, which he spits out. His resentment against his parents and God, and his need to blame someone, is never explained in the text, but simply left as negative concepts for young readers to take on board.

Before leaving the subject of the church, I must mention Geraldine McCaughrean's *A Little Lower than the Angels*. This is the story of Gabriel, an ex-mason's apprentice, who joins a company of medieval mystery players. I found here an accurate and sympathetic portrayal of the Christian faith, including some deep truths concerning the word of God. Pride and deception are exposed. Warnings are given about the taking of God's glory for oneself, and departing from the original words of the Bible in order to please the people. The villain meets with death but Garvey (playing the part of God) repents and is saved.

Though this book is fascinating and hard to put down, some aspects are disturbing. When "God" loses patience he exclaims, "Damn me!" Maybe this serves to remind us that he is only an actor. However, I wonder if it is used symbolically to emphasise a theme of blasphemy through out the novel?

Lucie who plays the part of "the devil" is really the hero! The story ends with the alarming statement "Izzie knew how the devil will look on the day of his redemption!" This is bound to lead to misunderstanding. The truth is that the devil will ultimately be sent to eternal hell (Rev. 20:10). Such confusion and the suggestion that the devil may be good is the subject of the next chapter.

More Recommended Books

For Younger Readers

The Very Worried Sparrow by M. Doney.

A Lion For the King   by   M. Doney.

The Hidden House.   by   M. Waddell.

 The Useless Donkeys.   by   L. Pender .

The Pencil and the Rubber by Peter Hellyer.

A Gift From Winklesea   by   H. Cresswell.

The Walls Come Tumbling Down by D. Hill.

For Older Readers

Narnia Series   by   C.S. Lewis.

Jeffey, the Burglar's Cat   by U.M. Williams.

The Silver Sword   by   I. Serraillier.

Pangur Ban, the White Cat by F. Sampson.

Message in a Bottle   by   Jenny Koralek.

The Bronze Bow   by   E. Speare.

Me, Jill Robinson   by   A. Digby.

Tom's Midnight Garden   by   P. Pearce.

Summer of the Zeppelin   by   E. McCutcheon.

 The Tanglewoods' Secret (and others) by P. St. John.

Chapter 3: <u>GOOD AND EVIL − THE COSMIC CONFRONTATION</u>

"Woe to those who call evil good and good evil,

who put darkness for light and light for darkness …"   (Isaiah 5:20)

A6) Is the traditional battle between good and evil clear or confused?

When Biggles and the Famous Five were in their heyday, before the moral decline of the 60's, it was taken for granted that the noble heroes, however ordinary, would triumph whilst the "baddies" would receive their just deserts. As in traditional tales, battle lines were clearly drawn between good and evil, whether in a fantasy setting or closer to home. One could expect the wicked witch to be evil, the giant to be frightening, even the naughty child to be shockingly bad, whilst authority figures like parents or policemen would at least be dependable and well-meaning and probably display admirable qualities.

That is not to say that a sinner could not be transformed by a change of heart, but his misdeeds were obvious to the reader. The humour of Billy Bunter or Dorothy Edwards' *My Naughty Little Sister* was largely due to our anticipation of trouble when the miscreants were caught.

Alison Uttley, author of the *Little Grey Rabbit* stories of the 1930s, wanted to "help children understand something of the moral choices and the difficulties that we all have to face", according to her biographer Dennis Judd. In each story she would hide a treasure: a legend, a proverb, a scrap of wisdom. She believed that "the world of the child should be a safe world, with good prevailing over evil". The differences between right and wrong were once defined by measuring against the standards of Christian teaching. The young reader would be encouraged to identify with the heroes and have a healthy hatred of the evil characters.

In modern stories these differences are no longer clear cut; the issues are clouded. Teenagers today have grown up during an age when role-models, fictional or otherwise, are unworthy of their status. Witches and wizards may be good or evil, dragons fearsome or friendly. We must ask ourselves, "Can it be right to confuse children about good and evil? Is such confusion beneficial to themselves or society?" Significantly, a recent expression of approval used by youngsters is, "That's wicked!" This adjective is being associated with notions of goodness, excitement and desirability – a connection which will be hard to erase.

From the beginning of history, there has been a cosmic confrontation in the spiritual realm between the two irreconcilable sides. If there is a conspiracy now to conceal it or deny it from children's experience, that only serves to prove its reality. In fact we could say that the deception is part of the enemy strategy; "part of the war that stretches out through the ages", in the words of Philip Dick in his science-fiction work *Nick and the Glimmung*.

There is no doubt in this case that the Glimmung, or devil figure, brings disorder and the curse of death to the land and its people, preying on their weaknesses. There is much spiritual insight in this book. Is it too fanciful then to imagine that Nick is symbolic of Jesus? He and his father, who have a very close relationship, arrive on a new planet with a vision for a wholesome future. They are attacked by evil creatures, and though Nick is made weak by the Glimmung's powerful gaze, he succeeds in maiming this devil forever. The Spiddles cry, "You have won a victory for us. You have saved us all."

When assessing children's fiction we must also ask, "What is the nature of the perceived evil that threatens?" If we delve a little deeper we may discover the "enemy" is not so bad. In fact it may be Christianity which is being resisted! In *The Dark is Rising* series by Susan Cooper, there is no assumption that Christianity is the force for good: the defeat of evil is intended to safeguard the status quo, pagan as that may be. This suggests either that there is an alternative beneficent power, or that Christianity per se is not good. *The Dark is Rising* boldly proclaims the message that paganism has the strongest power and existed before the battle between the church and the devil ever began. This of course is a deception, since God had planned from the beginning that Jesus, the head of the church, would defeat the devil and all his works.

The problem for children today is that they cannot be sure which characters *are* on the good side, and even if they think they know, they may be mistaken! With whom should the reader empathise? Are the heroes really the good ones, or are they in fact seeking help from the same evil powers as those of the enemy? Alan Garner, in his novel *Elidor*, calls his good prince by the malevolent-sounding name of Malebron. Is this a deliberate blurring of the edges?

In *The Moon of Gomrath* by the same author, the children make friends with the wizard and his elves, though the loyalties of these characters are never quite clear. The elves are "merciless without kindness", whilst "the eyes of a dwarf are born to darkness". Of course this could mean that dwarfs live constantly underground, but the symbolism of light and dark corresponding with good and evil is instinctively and universally known. (This is of spiritual significance and has nothing to do with the black and white of racial colour).

6.1) Are the symbols of dark and light used in the conventional way or reversed?

"God is Light; in Him there is no darkness at all" (1 John 1:5). Jesus urged us to be "children of light", being fruitful in "goodness, righteousness and truth" (Eph. 5:8,9). However Satan, the arch-counterfeit, is also known as Lucifer, or light-bearer, so the *source* of the light referred to in a story must be identified.

The wizard of Earthsea brought light to the blind man, and the light of Ogion his mentor was needed to dispel the dark spirit. However, this is magic light. When asked, "What other great powers are there besides the light?" Ged replies, "All power is one in source and end" and later muses," Maybe there is no true power but the dark". Thus we see that in modern children's books light is not necessarily good. What on the surface appears to be a battle between good and evil, may actually be evil versus evil, with the reader being deceived into thinking that one of these evils must be good.

Who is the enemy in Sheila McCullagh's *Tim and Tobias* (a 1970s school reading scheme now reprinted)? The electric light in Tim's bedroom never works when the magic cat Tobias is present. When the absence of light is used conventionally it symbolises covert activity and should be coupled with at least an implied warning to reject it, yet the main theme of this series is the friendship between Tim and the cat.

When Tim by choice is involved with the ghostly smugglers (Book A4), the policeman's torch renders Tim invisible, immune to detection. This light, which should reveal wickedness, symbolises instead the impotence of the law against magic, and of light over dark.

6.2) Is evil condemned and good seen to be victorious?

"Hate evil, love good …"   (Amos 5:15)

Though some may argue that in real life the villain often seems to win, nevertheless Jesus demonstrated the power of love over hate, truth over deceit. Aesop's Fable, *The North Wind and the Sun,* illustrates the victory of gentleness over violence. In the eternal time span good will always win because God is good! (Psalm 25:8). At a more domestic level, the benefits of teaching children that virtue is rewarded and wickedness punished are obvious. This is the way to a peaceful home and orderly society.

For good to be seen to triumph, evil must be condemned. Geraldine McCaughrean's beautifully presented *St.George and the Dragon* makes a very clear statement regarding the victory over evil. St.George, the pure man, in no uncertain way defeats the dragon whose "father was Evil, its mother darkness, and its name … wickedness".

Sadly, in junior fiction today the opposite is often the case. Rather than warning that evil situations are not to be entered into unless absolutely unavoidable, and that bad behaviour is not to be condoned, these alternative options appear to be more exciting. In Penelope Farmer's *Charlotte Sometimes*, Clare is described as "…fearfully holy … and good, horribly good".

Incredibly, in *Conrad, the Factory-Made Boy* by Christine Nostlinger, it is the mother herself who hates the word good. "It's as bad as … tidy or well-behaved" she says. Roles are reversed in this saga of a boy who arrives in a can by postal error, already programmed for perfect conduct on every occasion. Conrad's morality is a social handicap to him and unable to prevent him from being returned to the factory. He is rejected because he is too good!

It is left to those with fewer scruples to save the day by devising a stratagem. Success is achieved by persuading Conrad to behave so appallingly that neither the factory-manager nor the true parents (portrayed as the baddies) want anything to do with him. He is left wondering how he should behave in future. The message to readers is very clear: naughtiness solves the problem.

It would be worthwhile in assessing reading materials to note how much space is given in the text to ungodly themes. In a small but fascinating survey of comics by Rosanna Williams, it was discovered that many more phrases were included that describe evil than good. For example, in a copy of *Masters of the Universe* there were fifteen phrases of a darker nature (including "evil warriors", "black evil", "by the great darkness", "black art") compared with just four references to "heroic warriors". We may infer that these stories concentrate on the enemy forces. This means that absorption of vocabulary is weighted on the undesirable side.

When evil appears to dominate, it can suggest that goodness is rather sissy. What persuades an author to emphasise the demon hordes, whilst side-lining the all powerful God and his angels? Are they not all part of the spiritual battle?

The Wizard of Earthsea (and his readers too) is told by Serret that "only darkness can defeat the dark". Here is another false statement which reminds us of an accusation against Jesus. The teachers of the law said, "By the prince of demons he is driving out demons", but Jesus replied, "How can Satan drive out Satan?" (Mark 3:23-26). We might sigh with relief when Ged refutes Serret's statement, but only for a moment, since he produces a staff which blazes with "white mage fire that … drives away the darkness". So, what kind of light is it?

The belief that dark defeats dark is indeed pagan. It grows out of a primitive supposition that darker spirits are the most real and powerful. Heathen idols are made as ugly as possible. One can rely on them to accomplish "dirty deeds". In Book C7 of the *Tim and Tobias* series, the magic of the horrid, green-eyed Stump-People is stronger than that of the cat: "nastier" means "more powerful". Yet again we begin to understand how revolutionary was Jesus' teaching, that love defeats our enemies.

6.3) Are evil and darkness deemed to be necessary, or even good?

With the persuasion that evil is potent, various philosophies arise regarding its usefulness. This is the message of *The New House Villain* by Margaret Mahy. When Julia moves into a new house, she is fearful of the evil being that lives in a tree outside. He reproaches her, "We villains do a lot of good in a quiet way … It would be a dull world if everyone was virtuous". He begins to change her mind. Eventually she is so convinced of his value that she persuades her parents not to fell the tree! At the climax of the tale, the villain boasts of his strength and wickedness. "Well, that's OK!" shouts Julia.

In L'Engle's *A Wind in the Door,* "a strange dark Teacher", the mysterious Blajeny, whose hypnotic voice "drove away fear", says of his companion the Cherubim, "Do not be afraid. He won't hurt you". Like the serpent in the Garden of Eden, he whispers, "You will not surely die". One of his fellow "Teachers" is a black snake. Another is Doctor Colubra, a family friend whose name is the Latin for "snake".

Again, in *A Swiftly Tilting Planet* the same author returns to the theme. As her hero Charles Wallace travels back in time to the creation of the universe, she refers to "torrents of rain which covered the planet with healing darkness". If, symbolically, darkness is good, it follows that evil does not exist: therefore there is no such thing as sin and nothing can be wrong. This doctrine is expressed through the heroine, Meg, in a state similar to transcendental meditation. −

"… she saw nothing … Nothing was. She was not. There was no dark. There was no light … Then a surge of joy ... Darkness was, and darkness was good. As was light. Light and darkness dancing together, born together, born of each other, neither preceding neither following, both fully being, in joyful rhythm … the ancient harmonies were new and it was good. It was very good."

Compare these words with the beginning of Genesis where God spoke into the dark emptiness and created the light. He saw that it was very good and separated the light from the darkness (Gen.1:4,5,9). Later, when Jesus came as "the Light of the World", the darkness could not comprehend it (or gain control over it) (John1:2-4). What confusion is being sown in young minds by alternative ideas?

6.4) Does the book imply there are no absolutes – all is relative?

Relativism is in the ascendancy! All is relative; what is wrong for you may be right for me. Without Christian values, who is to say which is the better way. Whilst Tomi, in *Dragon Paths* (by F. Bloomfield) declares, "I would rather eat than worry about my honour", his father counters, "A man would rather kill himself than be dishonoured". Whether one or the other is right is debatable, though the reader would be led to agree with Tomi since he is the hero. The father admits the possibility of being wrong, but he does what seems right to him. How reminiscent of the people of Israel in the time of the Judges. With no king, each person did as he saw fit (Judges 21:25). The result was anarchy.

Without a standard to measure by it is as though the boundaries become ill-defined. In Rosa Guy's *The Friends*, the mother is heard to say hopelessly, "What I considered right and wrong have lost their distinction. Now, what I considered right is completely wrong, and what a short time ago I might have considered wrong is just the way of things."

Yet another strand in this tangled confusion is the old Chinese yin-yang theory arising from the belief that there are no absolutes. Evil is recognised, but is thought to have a little good in it, whilst goodness must contain a little evil. Notice also in stories, the prevalence of the colour or name "grey". In *The Winter Players*, Grey is the wolfish devil-figure who is eventually set free to be a nobleman with only "a smattering of sorcery".

Since Jesus acknowledged the reality of Satan, there is no reason why Christians should not. He told us that Satan is the father of lies, so when we are told that no-one is absolutely good, we must compare that with the Biblical truth that "the Lord is upright …there is no wickedness in him" (Ps.92:15). Likewise in the New Testament, St. John says of Jesus, "In Him is no sin" (1 Jn.3:5). In comparison, the Bible refers to Satan, whose name means adversary, as the wicked one (Matt.13:19 KJ), the opposer and enemy of God and his people (1 Peter 5:8).

Thus the yin-yang theory is contrary to Bible truth and its origins are questionable. It creeps subtly into children's books where we see the wicked witch with a good heart, one friendly giant amongst many ruffians, or a charm which can both help or harm. Philosophies following in its wake advocate the necessary balance between good and evil.

This is encapsulated in a clever play on words with the title Earthsea. Le Guin suggests that evil powers do not rise out of the sea but are of the earth. Thus this imaginary world is a blend of good and evil. Ged is impatient to drive back the darkness with his own "light", but the Master Wizard warns that "to light a candle is to cast a shadow", to make even a small change to part of the world is to upset the equilibrium of the whole. Who knows what will result?

L'Engle pursues the same theory. When Matthew says, in *A Swiftly Tilting Planet*, "Nothing, no-one is too small to matter", he is referring, not to our worth in God's sight, but to our place in the pattern of time and space! This writer intends her readers to delve for meanings under the surface. The cover blurb states: "We regain the perspective of the old mystics through the vision of modern science." Though presented as science-fiction, a spiritual atmosphere pervades the work, but it is not particularly Christian. Consider Meg's journey through the amber mandala-eye of the Cherubim (*A Wind in the Door*). Here is Hindu symbolism associated with the search for self-unity and universal completeness.

L'Engle and others convey the message that it is dangerous to upset this delicately balanced world: let it be – for you do not know what may happen if it is changed in any way! Yet *Jesus* came to change the world, to speak against complacency and to deal with the sin in the heart of mankind. He came to disturb, to challenge and to defeat the powers of darkness.

Goodness must be promoted as the more attractive option, the winning side, so that children will once again choose to champion righteousness. Beware of those who would declare a truce in the battle between good and evil! It is not a truce that is needed, nor even a peace-pact, but a declaration of the victory won by God's strategy!

More Recommended Books

For Younger Readers

St. George by G. McCaughrean.

Nick and the Glimmung by   Philip Dick.

Catchpole, King of the Castle by D. Oakden.

For Older Readers

The Farthest Away Mountain by L.R. Banks.

The Mouse Butcher   by   D.K. Smith.

Hagbane's Doom   by.   J. Houghton.

The Cloak   by   Patricia St.John.

The Guest   by   P. St.John.

Chapter 4: <u>NEW AGE INFLUENCES</u>

"Have nothing to do with the fruitless deeds of darkness, but rather expose them…."   (Ephesians 5:11)

A7) Are New Age ideas being infiltrated into young fiction?

Many of the points raised in the previous chapter are associated with the current teaching known as "New Age". This movement, which exudes spirituality, speaks of peace and harmony and even seems to awaken a God-consciousness, is actually a deception.

At the heart of the New Age is the Doctrine of Wholeness, or the interconnectedness of all things. "Science and occultism are placed on a par … good and evil no longer exist. All is one" writes Mother Basilea Schlink in *New Age From a Biblical Viewpoint*. New-Agers say "If all is good, then all religions are good". They promote syncretism and a "one world faith". There is deference to the gods rather than God. Eastern religions and even paganism are accommodated. New Age philosophy is not so much new as a hotch-potch of old ritual and occult blended together with modern packaging.

We find that certain symbols, hitherto harmless, such as rainbows, crystals and unicorns, now carry New Age overtones because they are associated with mysticism. When Charles Wallace of *A Swiftly Tilting Planet* calls upon the help of "all heaven with is power" to intervene, because the survival of this planet is under threat, who should appear but Gaudior, a unicorn with a crystal horn. His use of exclamations like "Thank the galaxies" and "Praise the music" give important clues regarding his orientation.

Because the New Age encourages relativism, all religions are warmly embraced, except Christianity. This is a distortion of multi-faith tolerance. The reason is that Jesus, the Word of God, proclaims absolutes. There is no place for God's absolute standards of right and wrong in the New Age.

At best, Christianity is only nominally acknowledged and Jesus seen as one of many prophets or teachers. The supposed "angels" of *A Wrinkle in Time* (refer to *Secret Messages* chapter 2, section 4.2), quoting John 1:5, encourage the children to name Jesus as one who has fought evil and been a light (rather than the light) in the darkness. They are then urged to name others who have been similar lights: "All your great artists − They've been lights for us to see by". Their list of fifteen includes Shakespeare, Michelangelo, Bach, Einstein, Ghandi and Buddha!

In such books we discern undercurrents from eastern religion. In *The Moon of Gomrath,* Albanac does not die, but is reincarnated into a different being. His time is up at the howl of a dog. Colin, the hero, speaks the truth when he says, "It makes everything so pointless."

For Oaive of *The Winter Players* we sense a similar frustration as she exclaims, "It is endless, Grey. We are caught in a wheel of time, turning forever". She feels trapped in life, in history. She dares to break the circle by going back in time to change the pattern, but this is no real comfort. According to this philosophy, the cycle will begin again. Compare Hebrews 9:27 in the Bible which clearly states that "man is destined to die once and after that to face judgement."

A similar theme occurs in *A Swiftly Tilting Planet* when the hero lives five other lives through historical characters. This however is more akin to the New Age phenomenon of transpersonal psychology, which involves allowing oneself to be manipulated by a psycho-technician, laying aside one's own personality in order to return to a previous existence.

7.1) Is there any reference to mind power, telepathy, E.S.P., etc.?

Having made herself giddy trying to pray, Laura of *The Finding* takes the major's advice to let her mind go blank and concentrate on her lost brother. By psychic knowledge she "sees" him and is given instructions for finding him. "Prayer concentrates the mind," says the major, who then proceeds to convince the reader that this mystical mind-power is more effective than Christian prayer. Eastern meditation and every kind of mind-power feature prominently in New Age teaching.

A convention used by writers is to ensure that their particularly important messages are delivered by characters with credibility in the eyes of the readers, perhaps a doctor or a teacher or, as in *Blubber* by Judy Blume, the school swat who believes in E.S.P. and reincarnation. In *The Shadow Guests*, the aunt's views on the paranormal must be logical because she is a mathematics professor. Of course the most influential characters are the heroes.

In Cooper's *Greenwitch*, Merryman and Will communicate by the power of the mind, a practice that L'Engle develops to the ultimate in *The Wind in the Door*. Meg and Charles Wallace excel in the art of "kything". The Cherubim tells them, "Open yourself to me so that I can open the door to your mind". Her books give detailed instructions in telepathy: how to kythe not only with people, but with angelic or demonic beings, with stars, leaves, even salt in the sea. The black snake uses visual projections.

In *The Winter Players*, we find allusions to astral travel and Oaive uses mind-power over the elements. Here, dreams foreshadow reality, as in *Greenwitch* where it is difficult to separate the two worlds. Rosa, heroine of *Black Nest* by Rachel Dixon, is troubled by bad dreams. She senses through them an outside influence from an unknown force which compels her to action.

7.2) Are the heroes influenced by spirit-guides?

Thus we find the presence of spirit-guides in works of so-called fantasy. Heroes are in communication with extraordinary beings beyond themselves, from other dimensions of space and time, from higher planes of existence. L'Engle's work gives obvious examples: Mrs Who, Mrs Which and Mrs Whatsit and the three beasts of Uriel, in *A Wrinkle in Time*; Gaudior in *A Swiftly Tilting Planet*; and in *A Wind in the Door*, Blajeny the "Teacher", together with the Cherubim who speaks directly into the mind, both of whom have been "sent", but by whom? Blajeny derives his wisdom from "some deep dark place within himself, and then further ... moving in, in, deeper and deeper, for time out of time".

The belief in "masters of wisdom" is basic to New Age doctrine and has its origins in the Theosophical Society from the nineteenth century. Its members were guided by mystical beings, either demonic spirits or specially gifted humans of unusual knowledge. It still thrives today. In L'Engle's books, the hero is super-intelligent. Blajeny says to him, "You are called ... invited to study with one of the "Teachers". The call appeals to his pride. Could he be a channeller of supernatural power?

The four heroes of *Master of Fiends* are described as talented: Archer whose mind can move material obstacles; Scythe who has inner mental vision; Mandra with power to affect the minds of others; Jarral possessing extraordinary inner power. They are humans using, "not magic but natural powers of the mind". "Splendid stuff", enthuses a School Librarian publication.

In a more familiar setting, Roald Dahl's child prodigy, Matilda, develops the ability to channel power through her eyes in order to upset her teacher by moving objects around. The child reader receives the message, "This is possible, even for you". Combine this with the concept of self-realisation and dependence on one's own power and we find the Hindu (and New Age) belief in the god within us: we are all gods.

7.3) Is there any reference to self-realisation?

Self-realisation is the ultimate of seven chakras, energy centres within the body, according to eastern religion. Does Meg achieve this goal when she steps through the Cherub's mandala eye into the "ultimate night on the other side", or does she in fact find the emptiness of Nirvana − the release from karma which is eternal death?

Throughout two of these books with a New Age flavour, *A Wind in the Door* and *A Wizard of Earthsea*, the philosophy of "naming" is pursued. Both authors teach that to name anything is the equivalent of ownership, of power over or intimacy with that person or object. Ged spends his apprenticeship with the Master Namer, learning the true name of every place, thing and being, "for magic consists of this". A god-like power is available to him! This way of life is bound to result in a suspicion of all new acquaintances and lying about one's true identity.

On the other hand, the Cherubim claims that "If someone knows who he is, really knows, then he doesn't need to hate". That may sound all very well, even spiritual, but then he goes on, "That's why we still need Namers … When everyone is really and truly named the (demons) will be vanquished". Here we have reference to specially called super-heroes again, now taking a god-like status. Naming may indeed indicate ownership, but only by the creator. The Cherubim speaks of naming the stars, but God the Creator has already named his universe −

"He who brings out the starry host one by one and calls them each by name..." (Isaiah 40:26).

− God who says, "He who created you, O Jacob, he who formed you O Israel, fear not for I have redeemed you, I have summoned you by name, you are mine." (Isaiah 43:1)

Only God has the right of ownership over his creation (Psalm 24:1), yet because of his love and compassion he has not bound us like slaves under his power, but given us free will. He desires us to freely choose to be called by *his* name. There is even the promise of a new divine name to those who are overcomers (Rev. 2:17b).

God has delegated responsibility to us, through Adam, for the naming of our children, animals and possessions. In this we are expected to be good stewards of his gifts entrusted to our care, following his example of discipline with love. Notice that in the well-known story of the Good Shepherd (John10), the sheep follow their Master, not because he has named them but because they know his voice (v.3-5). We need to recognise the difference between the deceiver's voice and the Word of Truth which is Jesus.

When an evil spirit recognised and named Jesus in the synagogue (Mark 1:24), it was promptly cast out with a shriek. There is no doubt whose power was greater. The name of *Jesus* holds divine power because it symbolises his victory over evil on the cross. It is given to those who follow him, not to hold power over Jesus, but over his enemy Satan.

Le Guin combines the theories of naming and yin-yang to bring Ged's story to a climax. He finally comes face to face with the evil shadow which has pursued him relentlessly. He pronounces its name, only to discover that it shares his own name, "…the black self … light and darkness met and joined and were one". He cries, "I am whole, I am free". In his self-realisation, he boasts self-sufficiency, in that he "cannot be used or possessed by any power other than himself".

This is totally different from Christianity. Jesus taught that his truth would set us free (John 8:32), and that true fulfilment is achieved when we become alive spiritually by his Holy Spirit (John 3:5). At that moment, darkness and sin are rejected and God's Spirit is invited to take charge of the believer's life. Out of a thankful heart, Christians pray to be used in God's service.

7.4) Are there signs of paganism or witchcraft?

Another thread woven into the tapestry of New Age is that of paganism and witchcraft. An element common to both is the seeking after power. Winkie Pratney, writing for parents in *Devil Take the Youngest*, explains that occultists aim to find the centre of secret power by going against the tide, against the natural, to find the source. "Reversal is the law of the satanic world. Works of darkness are unnatural". Bearing this in mind makes it easier to understand a rather strange passage from *A Wizard of Earthsea*:

"A man would know the end he goes to, but he cannot know it if he does not turn, and return to his beginning and hold that beginning in his being … Now turn clear around and seek the very source, and that which lies before the source. There lies your hope of strength."

Is this describing the circle symbol − the serpent with the tail in its mouth, which is everything but nothing, round and round forever, but never going anywhere? Could this be an example of what the reviewer in the Times Educational Supplement meant when he wrote of Le Guin's trilogy: "We are ready for new parables and here they are … completely convincing … compulsory reading". Let us hope that such fiction never becomes compulsory reading!

That paganism is alive and well is evident from the number of websites devoted to it. Paganism is thought to be the fastest growing religion in the UK (Telegraph 2014). In an article in *The Pagan News* (1989) entitled *All-In Vayne – Occult Primers*, the writer urges fellow occultists to promote their beliefs through children's fiction, following the example of many established authors, many of whom are women. He observes, "As an occultist, I often feel that the authors must be directly involved with magick themselves".

He goes on "Those (readers) who feel an instinctive interest will wish to investigate the mysteries in more depth, while those who simply enjoy a good story will at least come to know the symbolism of magick and be more open-minded and tolerant as a result". Such sentiments give us strong grounds for concern regarding the conditioning of children's minds.

Women are central to pagan themes. At the climax of *Master of Fiends* the sword carried into the enemy kingdom is really a female spirit. In *Spellhorn*, by B. Doherty, a unicorn carries Laura away to a primitive place inhabited by the Wild Ones, sun-worshippers under the leadership of the matriarchal Old Woman. Though the land is called the Wilderness, the meaning of the word has been reversed: "The world lit up for Laura". It is portrayed as beautiful, colourful, exciting. In the centre is a cave – the dark eye of the Wilderness. Note also that it is a Mrs Grey who provides the information about unicorns, that their horns were used for healing and that they belonged to "a better time".

In the oldest, and by implication truest, forms of goddess-worship there would be a female trinity ruling cycles of creation, birth and death, symbolised by a virgin, mother and crone. Pratney has traced back the counterfeit virgin and child symbols to the ancient mystery religion of Babylon. The Tower of Babel is said to have been designed by Nimrod to focus occult power. When he died, his wife, Semiramis (also known as Artemis or Diana), announced that the king had returned from self-sacrifice in the form of her son, Tammuz. Nimrod became deified as the sun-god, or Baal (female counterpart was Ashera), associated with fertility, sexual immorality, dying and rising as in nature and child sacrifice.

In J.H.Brennan's story of *Shiva* and its sequel *The Crone*, it is clear that paganism, witchcraft and psychic activity all stem from the same origins and are inter-related. Here we see worship of the sun and mother goddess, and evidence of a female trinity: the Crone, Renka the tribal leader, and the virgin Shiva. The Crone practises "dark witchcraft". By means of trance-inducing potions she gains superior psychic, or magical, knowledge. The reader is told that "blood magic (is) potent" and that human sacrifice, like women's magic, is associated with great power.

The tribe believe in god-like ancestor spirits and reincarnation. They celebrate the Midsummer Solstice, "calling on its ancestors, its totem beasts and tribal gods for aid". The Crone practices divination with tellstones and uses the power of her spirit-guide, a Crow.

With a return to pagan ideas, it is not surprising that there is a liberal scattering of runes amongst the pages of children's books. Runes may merely signify an ancient alphabet, but they do hold associations with magic and spells. In *A Swiftly Tilting Planet* there is repeated use of runes in the form of rhyming spells, calling on help from the sun, snow, fire and sea for protection from evil. When urging Zillah to sail for Vespugia, Matthew quotes Isaiah 43:2:

"When you pass through the waters I will be with you, and when you pass through the rivers they will not sweep over you. When you walk through the fire you will not be burnt; the flames will not set you ablaze", and then adds, "For the fire is roses, roses".

The line that should have followed is "For I am the Lord your God, the Holy One of Israel, your Saviour". In omitting this statement and substituting a pagan one, it has the effect of changing the scripture into a rune! The words are used as an acknowledgement of their religious power, but the lordship of God has been removed.

Le Guin refers to the runes and the "Old Speech" as a path to understanding which sounds suspiciously akin to gnosticism – the acquiring of secret knowledge. One is reminded of the priceless Book of Gramarye in *The Dark is Rising*, given to Will by the Old Ones (his Masters). It was "a book of hidden things… of the real magic … our business was called simply knowing".

7.5) Is there reference to the "old religion"?

Back in 1950 when C.S. Lewis wrote in *The Lion, the Witch and the Wardrobe* of the "Deep Magic from the Dawn of Time", it was understood that he referred to the eternal laws laid down by God from the beginning that cannot be broken (Ps.119:89-91). Even the White Witch could demand Edmund's death as a right in order to satisfy the old law. When Aslan stepped in to take the sinner's place, he was fulfilling the requirement of the unchangeable "magic", yet at the same time bringing in God's saving grace. Lewis obviously did not foresee that for a future generation of children, the word magic would be more commonly associated with the occult than with mystery.

Reference to the "old magic" or the "old religion" *now* in junior fiction invariably means pagan activity and is promoted as the original, and therefore true, teaching. The suggestion that it claims our allegiance by its authenticity is woven into *The Guardian of Isis* by Monica Hughes. Even though this is science-fiction, again we find an emphasis on religious symbolism. The writer asserts that the Elders, originally inhabitants of Earth, have the real truth. The reader might assume that these folk adhere to the fundamental Christian faith, whist the *second* generation on Isis have abandoned the truth. However, when all is revealed, it becomes clear that those scorned and condemned as "deceivers" are actually *Christians.*

What religion is it then that the Elders cling to? The clues come from Lady Olwen, the Keeper of the Light and the voice of "wisdom". She and the Elders are given credibility because of the support of the hero, Jody, who considers her green snake-like appearance attractive. Olwen declares, "God made the universe and everything in it. And there is no destroyer" (cf. Exodus 12:23). In saying this she is denying the existence of the devil. "Death is a friend," she says, "only a door to a new and beautiful land" – a universal salvation?

This is pagan witchcraft: disbelief in Satan, upholding the old religion, the worship of the divine in nature, animal-loving, environmentally conscious and promoting an image of harmless simplicity. In fact it is a modern form of Babylonian worship of the divine mother, a fertility cult which grows best in advanced but Godless civilisations. Now known as Wicca, its followers cast spells and invoke deities such as the Great Mother Diana. Those who follow pagan religion claim that Christians are the interlopers who have violated their sacred altars and attacked their followers. Christians are accused of taking over these "high places" and planting churches there.

Bearing this is in mind, who are the "victims of evil and injustice" that Rose, as the Messenger of Favour, the great *grey* horse, is sent to rescue in *Cry of a Seagull*? Why should one suspect Monica Dickens of using pagan themes? We must look at the clues. Is Favour, the Messenger, merely the imaginary companion of a horse-lover, or in fact a spirit-guide? He is alive for all time, a secret supernatural being that controls Rose's life. Mind-power and visual projection are hinted: "she made her mind and eyes go blank to try to project herself into that other fantastic half of the double life she led". Rose is taunted by an evil lord in the fantasy world. Bravely she speaks out, "The forces of light are stronger than the forces of darkness!" However, the lord is left with the last word when he falsely declares, "But the light can be extinguished"!

7.6) Does the book preach one world government and peace?

Integral to paganism and witchcraft is the worship of Ea, Gaia or Mother Earth. The Wizard of Earthsea drew his power from the earth, whilst L'Engle speaks of the rhythm of the earth as if it is alive. The underlying theme of her *A Wind in the Door* is that of human cells being microcosms of the total person, and people as microcosms of the whole planet, which is a living organism. As such, New-Agers consider it worthy of worship – a deified planet – and not just the planet but the whole galaxy. Unfortunately this theme is infiltrating the environmental groups and green issues. Its implications will be dealt with in greater depth in chapter 7.

With the concept of the world as a unit, we come full circle to the New Age doctrine of wholeness: the world is one community, united in harmony, not only accepting all religions but one religion for all, under the control of one-world government. Even now we hear political leaders using New Age jargon, speaking of "a new world order".

Charles Wallace (hero of *A Swiftly Tilting Planet*) sees in the scrying pool a picture of "a blue-eyed baby, the answer to prayer who is to bring peace". A new but false messiah perhaps? The Red-Indian folk-lore of Zylle in the same story is presented as more peace-loving than the religion of the Puritan settlers. The pastor is criticised for not respecting the Indian gods. Zylle sings, "Come from fathers long gone by, bring blue from a distant eye". Reference is being made to the belief that some Red-Indians have Welsh ancestors from whom come blue eyes and second sight.

Blue eyes figure so prominently, e.g. Charles Wallace himself, Olwen the *Guardian of Isis*, Laura of *Spellhorn*, that one suspects shades of the Aryan super-race theory, (or even "masters of wisdom"), especially when combined with blond hair as a sign of privileged nobility as in *The Golden Journey* by J.R.Townsend. Blue-eyed Eleni sets out on a journey intended to bring peace to her world. She is called as a "Messenger of the Living God", though the deity described here is only a caricature of God. She finds she has aristocratic connections and is eventually given a divine spirit. Peace is achieved, with the concluding message that Eleni believed in herself more than anything else.

Though the *Book of Revelation* is difficult and controversial, many agree that it points to the coming of an Anti-Christ about whom Jesus warned us. He is expected to be a world leader empowered by "the dragon" (Rev.13:2), that ancient serpent called Satan (Rev.12:9).He will demand obeisance and lead a world government hailing peace. Peace between men and dragons, with the promise of a better world, is the theme of *The Dragons of North Chittendom* by Susan Fromburg. Should we make peace with dragons? Jeremiah prophesied, "Peace, peace, they say, when there is no peace" (Jer.6:14).

Christians believe there can be no real peace without Jesus. He is the Prince of Peace and he warned us against deception. The devil's aim is to keep his strategies hidden from public awareness. By persuading our minds to accept as normal those things which are not of God, even young children are being conditioned. They will become so familiar with the New Age symbolism being absorbed through literature, that they will not be aware of deception as the onslaught increases. They will be oblivious to the warning signs.

Since most titles in this chapter have been for older or more proficient readers, I will conclude with some comments on a book for younger children: *Tatty Apple*, by Jenny Nimmo. Here we see all the characteristics previously described, woven into one simple "fantasy". On the cover is a rainbow cleverly drawn to link the heads (or minds) of the hero and heroine. Owen Owens, who enjoys dragons on his bedroom wall-paper, lives in a land where everything is green – Wales no doubt.

The cover blurb describes Tatty Apple, the green rabbit, as making "the most wonderful magic of all". This pet uses mind-power to move objects for no apparent reason, a talent which is kept secret from mum who would not approve. The rabbit is portrayed as helper, saviour and healer, using mysterious psychic powers. Finally he makes a rainbow of flowers in the sky and chases away after it, never to return. However, Owen Owens knows that they will "always be able to find Tatty Apple up there in the high woods and fields when they need him most". Is the spiritual symbolism coincidental?

We need to remain alert, praying for discernment about the signs of the times, as Jesus warned us; praying also for protection from confusion and dulling of the mind. There are many who wish to promote their own philosophies and superstitions, whether overtly New Age or otherwise. Let us beware, for the children's sake, of what is happening. Such teaching, if not of God, can only be harmful.

Chapter 5:   <u>VALUES FOR LIFE</u>

"You are my friends if you do what I command."   (John 15:14)

B) Is Christian teaching endorsed or contradicted?

B 1) Are Christian values upheld?

In the West, countless generations have enjoyed a valuable treasure, the inheritance of the early Christianisation of their lands. Through the ages people have fought, rightly or wrongly, to maintain justice and freedom in the name of Christ. In Britain, the Biblical values that we have stood for and hold dear have formed the foundation of our moral code, indeed the backbone of our parliamentary constitution, for which we have earned respect from other cultures.

Some would consider themselves Christians purely on the basis of adherence to the teachings of Jesus. Such ideals as the pursuit of truth, the keeping of promises, fair dealing, self-control over passions of love and hate − all have a scriptural origin and have been promoted even by non-Christians for their good sense and practicality, in keeping with a civilised way of life.

In the current climate of assertiveness and independence of thought, there are those who talk about the "post-Christian era" as though it were a good reason to overturn convention and open the doors to a new morality. *The Guardian of Isis* delivers the message that to abandon taboos and restrictions leads to a better, more genuine way of life. Whilst throwing out Christianity, many have turned to other faiths or embraced humanism − a devotion to human interests that is close to a religion in itself!

Because of this influence over the past fifty years, today's parents have been conditioned to accept secular values as normal. Though they may not personally put these into practice, they are now more likely to tolerate the resulting behaviour in the younger generation. One way in which these alternative lifestyles have been taught is through story books.

In chapter two we considered the question, "Is God present in fiction by implication?" His presence may be measured by the degree of importance given to Christian values. In the past children's classics have majored on such virtues as integrity, loyalty, courage and discipline. Traditional folk-tales have been the vehicle for promoting personal attributes like humility, patience and perseverance. But where does today's young reader find these themes?

Certainly there are some praiseworthy titles like *The Bronze Bow* (Elizabeth Speare) and *Treasures of the Snow* (P.St.John), in which we read of victory won through courage, trust, friendship and forgiveness. Such books though are swamped by a vast sea of unremarkable material and are seldom seen on the shelves of any but Christian bookshops. Authors of this kind need to be encouraged, for the children's sake.

Ann Lawrence's *Merlin the Wizard* disparages himself as a fool to "love another more than myself". Whereas he feels this love to be a restriction which will bind him forever, the selfless quality of *Christian* love has a liberating effect. Another strange idea comes from L'Engle's Cherubim who reckons that when you feel hatred you can be restored to rightness by thinking of someone you love! Is that really the truth?

Compare these false messages with the truths that Patricia St. John delivers. Terror-stricken Lebanon is the setting for *Nothing Else Matters*. The mother says wisely that faith is best protected "in a heart that loves and forgives", not by hate and revenge. Her daughter, Lamia, discovers that "hating is a lonely business, a private hell". Answers come through her friend, who reveals the truth that knowing the love and forgiveness of Jesus frees us to do the same for others.

This author opens up a genuine discussion as Amin grapples with a dilemma: the tension between his loyalty to his friend, whose family are on the enemy side, and the matter of obedience to his parents. This friendship leads to his abduction and death. He had not asked his parents' permission to visit the boy's house, deceiving his mother and ignoring the advice of a Christian friend. The key question raised is, "Loyalty to whom?"

Children must be taught to prioritise their loyalties. The heroes of *Greenwitch* condemn a man for informing on his friend. "He's the town's shame", says Captain Tom. However, that friend just happens to be a murderer. This suggests that hindering the course of justice is excusable when friendship is at stake.

Ironically, the thirty-two titles of the *Tim and Tobias* reading scheme, encompassing a theme of occult and horror with a certain amount of deceit thrown in, reveal a positive attitude to keeping one's word. Tim's ghostly friend warns that promises "have to be kept even when they're made to your enemies". This is yet another aspect of the blend of good and bad. Great care is needed when choosing books for children, regarding the values for life that they will unwittingly learn.

1.1) Is bad behaviour presented as entertainment?

In complete contrast with those who either condemn dishonourable behaviour, or seek to justify it as necessary in certain circumstances, there are some writers who intend to *entertain* readers by their heroes' shockingly bad deeds. Would that all might hold the same aims as Eileen Colwell, compiler of *Bad Boys*, who acknowledges: "It was difficult to find stories with the right degree of naughtiness. I avoided purely destructive behaviour and looked for the element of fantasy which made for variety and fun which was not likely to be emulated by the children listening".

Of course there have been notorious anti-heroes who have endeared themselves to us, like Richmal Crompton's *William*. However, he seems a far cry from Little Dracula who, having been tucked up in his cosy coffin, whispers wistfully in his mother's ear, "When I grow up I'll be horrible and nasty like you and dad, won't I?" (*Little Dracula at the Seaside* by Martin Waddell). One of the revolting pastimes in which he and his family indulge is to play tennis using flattened cats as rackets. I was exceedingly alarmed to find this book both in the toddlers' picture-book box in the library and on the shelves of my local Special Needs Resource Centre which is part of the education service.

In a similar vein, readers of the role-playing fantasy *Monster Horrorshow* are enticed, for entertainment's sake, with the promise of "…accumulating gold and generally behaving in a totally disgraceful manner"! The reader expects the "bad guy" to be suitably nasty, even wicked, but when it is the hero, or another major character who crosses the boundaries of acceptability then one needs to see elements of reproof, repentance and retribution, if only implied.

Yet virtue, it seems, is out of fashion. We could be persuaded that vice is far more exciting. Rather than heed St.Paul's words from Philippians 4:8 – "Whatsoever things are true… noble… right… pure… lovely… admirable… excellent or praiseworthy… think about such things…", many writers would persuade us that the opposite qualities are more realistic and that youngsters must not be shielded from them. Well, that is an arguable point. Hunger, sickness, violence and war are realities but loving parents would not willingly expose their offspring to such things just for the experience!

B2) Is blasphemy, swearing and other bad language regarded as normal, necessary or excusable?

This section contains material that is neither pure nor lovely, yet because these examples have been collected from children's books, I feel it necessary to give adults the complete picture. You are free to skip these passages but remember that your children will neither skip nor ignore them. They may derive illicit pleasure from reading such material, or alternatively find it embarrassing. If however they are accustomed to vulgarity at home or at school, meeting it through the written word will serve to establish in the young mind its acceptability in society. In any case, each time a child reads these words, he will be saying them to himself, absorbing them at a sub-conscious level, and is more likely to use them in conversation.

Blasphemy directly or indirectly detracts from the glory and honour of God. It is defined in the Oxford Dictionary as "impious or profane speaking" and would describe the quotes in this section. The popular understanding of the term is "the taking of God's name in vain" (Exodus 20:7).

In my survey I have encountered several instances of heroes and heroines using the name of God as an expletive. *In Rob's Place* by J.R. Townsend, Dad exclaims, "God give me strength!", though the rest of his lifestyle as a gambler and drinker has no regard for God. Even Mike, the clean-cut, responsible type gasps, "Christ, it's young Rob!" as he rushes to rescue him from drowning at the island. Amongst the many authors who use similar expletives are Rosa Guy, Susan Cooper, Robert Westall, Penelope Lively, Phil Redmond, Ann Ruffell and David Angus.

The word "damn" may be classified by the Oxford Dictionary merely as "colloquial", yet when it features in a child's vocabulary one cannot help but feel disappointed. After all, it is a form of verbal curse, as is the use of the word "hell". These words are used freely in works by Nina Bawden, Vivien Alcock, Joan Aiken, Louise Lawrence, Rosa Guy, to name a few. They come from the lips of heroes, heroines, their families and friends. In role-playing books like *Seas of Blood*, it is the *reader* as hero who exclaims, "Damn me to the seven hells if I'll let you take her El-Fazouk". Even in a book like *Dog Powder*, which Mary Hoffman intended for young readers, we find the expression, "There's been hell to pay here".

It is often argued that "strong" words are excusable in certain circumstances to add to the authenticity of the lifestyles described. Why then, in *The Finding*, is it the father who mutters, "Damn the woman" and a passing motor-cyclist who shouts, "Bloody young half-wit", yet no bad language is spoken by the rough company Alex keeps when he runs away to a squat in London?

Swearing and bad language are abusive and obscene; neither would measure up to St.Paul's standards. In writing to the Colossians, he urges them to rid themselves of filthy language, whist Jesus taught that it is the indecency that comes out of a person's heart that makes one unclean (Mark 7:22). The use of the word "bloody" is becoming so common that one senses the shock diminishing the more one meets it. It is infiltrating children's language processes through novels in which they identify with the heroes, seeing them as role-models. Most of the authors mentioned above use this word or its euphemisms without shame. Here are a few examples:

"Now the bloody thing has gone out". (Heroine's guardian in *Voices* by J.Aiken).

"Bloody Helen"   (Rob, of his baby sister in *Rob's Place*).

"It's a ruddy great tree"   (*Tatty Apple*).

In *A Very Positive Moment* by Tim Kennemore, the word "bloody" is used by the 12-year –old heroine three times in as many pages.

To widen the vocabulary, here is a further selection:

Friendly neighbour: "Stupid little bugger". (*On the Lion's Side* by Ann Pilling)

Heroine, of teacher: "the bitch". (*Blubber* by Judy Blume)

Heroine: "I didn't effing start it!"   (*Frankie's Dad* by Jean Ure)

"I think it's a crock of shit"   (*Anastasia Krupnik* by Lois Lowry)

This book, in large print, is for a youngish reader, say 9-11. Other titles for a similar or lower age-range, though less explicit, still refer to swearing. On the second page of Sheila Lavelle's *The Big Stink*, we find the hero muttering a bad word under his breath, "the one his dad said sometimes when he bashed his thumb with a hammer". Surely even allusions to children swearing are unnecessary in beginner books. It reinforces the idea of normal practice in order to express feelings of frustration, even rebellion, as well as angry abuse. There is little attempt to widen a child's expressive vocabulary in more edifying ways.

Maybe some adults would support the mother of *Blubber*'s heroine who considers herself to be far-sighted and wise in allowing her daughter to swear. Her theory is that anything forbidden, kids will want to do even more. Similarly, the family in *Yaxley's Cat* (by Robert Westall) entertain themselves playing Dirty Scrabble. Is it any wonder that they use revolting language quite gratuitously in everyday conversation? This attitude is in complete contrast with the Biblical principles of parental and self discipline.

B3) Are rudeness and vulgarity a) allowed to go unchallenged, b) used to attract readership, or c) used gratuitously?

Particular mention should be made to Roald Dahl who is less likely to use common swear-words, but prefers an inventive approach, developing his own brand of verbal vulgarity. In *The B.F.G.*, the giant describes his staple diet of snozzcumber as "filthing, disgusterous, sickable, maggot-wise and foulsome", tasting of "frogfilth and pigsquibble". Giant Bloodbottler calls the B.F.G. a "runty little scumscrewer, a prunty little pogswizzler … dotty as a dogswoggler".

Another of Dahl's efforts, *The Witches*, was given the Whitbread Award for being "deliciously disgusting … a real book for children". Do judge for yourself! There is much about dogs' droppings and stinky children. The smell of the High Witch's bedroom is the same as "the inside of the men's public lavatory", whilst Mr. Jenkins says of his son, "He suffers from wind. You should hear him after supper. He sounds like a brass band." Indeed, Dahl seems to have a pre-occupation with this ailment, as he devotes a whole chapter to it in *The B.F.G.*, despite clearly stating that it is not a polite subject! More will be exposed regarding Dahl's vulgar humour in chapter 11.

There are some authors for whom nothing is taboo; any subject may be mentioned, even those which might not necessarily be vulgar, but merely private. Judy Blume is notoriously uninhibited. On the first page of *Blubber* the girls are ogling at pictures of naked bodies and by the third page we find a description of nose-picking.

In *Are You There God?*, girls' anatomical development is discussed in the first chapter, together with the art of kissing. Margaret's eventual breakthrough into womanhood at the long-awaited age of twelve forms the climax of the book, when she feels so good that she condescends to resume her talks with God! There is similar frankness in Cynthia Voight's *Come a Stranger*, though without the intent to shock.

Finally, before leaving this distasteful section, let us look briefly at the alternative meaning of "rudeness". When Tim throws a snowball down Miss Miff's neck (*Tim and Tobias, Bk.A3*), there is no sign of an apology. He is merely told by his mother to keep out of the old lady's way for a while!

In *The Finding*, Laura petulantly sticks her tongue out and makes a rude noise at Mrs. Angel's visitor. The reader empathises with the girl. The same lack of courtesy is shown in Margaret Stuart Barry's book *The Witch V.I.P.* when the headmaster retorts, "Nobody's asking you for your pocket-money, little Miss Clever-Clogs."

There is a general attitude of disrespect creeping in that will be discussed further in the next chapter. The age-old problem of the human heart that distances us from God is simply self-centredness – putting one's own interests and feelings before others. Even swearing and vulgarity have their roots in selfishness. As we assert ourselves and flout convention, we rebel against decency. The writer of the ancient book of Numbers (15:30-31) wisely observed:

"… Anyone who sins defiantly …blasphemes the Lord …because he has despised the Lord's word".

B4) Does the book portray selfishness, greed or materialism?

We will continue to look at some examples of characters who sin defiantly without any correction and without feeling remorse for their attitudes. First though let us consider selfishness.

There is a little book called *Dinner Ladies Don't Count* which illustrates the "I want" syndrome. Jason is in a temper because his mother will not let him have a dog. He translates his feelings into rebellious deeds at school. Author Bernard Ashley strives to explain the *reason* for the naughtiness but he does not make it clear that disappointment is no excuse for anti-social behaviour, nor does he suggest better ways of dealing with it.

Selfishness is fuelled by over-indulgent parents. The 9-year-old hero of *Dog Powder* has bought a collar, a lead and a medallion for his imaginary pet. He obviously receives large amounts of pocket-money, for he is saving up for a proper dog's bed too. In *The Key to the Other* by Anna Lewins, Flip longs to buy even the things he does not need.

The accumulation of useless articles is the subject of Russell Hoban's *Ponders* in which he describes life on the pond. What makes Big John Turkle happier than catching a duck for supper? It is the satisfaction of knowing that he, and not Grover Crow, has possession of the willow-patterned cup-handle. He has coveted it ever since the crow snobbishly boasted of his "objet d'art". Having stolen the piece of china, it is no good to him, except to his ego. Yes, a good message, but will the readers of picture books understand the irony?

Envy and materialism inevitably lead to greed. This vice is encouraged in the role-playing book *Seas of Blood*, in which the reader must by "ruthless greed" and "daring raids" , win the most gold and so prove himself the greatest pirate. There are no rules! An alternative outlet for self-indulgence is gluttony. The happiest solution Ted Hughes can supply for *The Iron Man*'s problem is that of a scrap-yard heaven with an unlimited diet of scrap-metal: "And he ate, ate, ate, ate, – endlessly"!

Surprisingly, Tim Kennemore has chosen the title *A Very Positive Moment* for his story about a gambling racket for 12-year-olds who could not otherwise afford fashionable clothes. "Crafty little Gillian" is taking bets on the winner of the election for form captain. Tamsin plans her own money-making scheme in the middle of the R.I. lesson, likening it to the principle of the loaves and fishes! She decides to beat Gillian at her own game by cheating her. The underlying, but well-stated message is, "If she's making money out of me, why shouldn't I take advantage of her". She appears to be well justified.

A detailed description of both schemes makes them easy to copy by readers. Even though both plans fail to make the expected wealth ("Tamsin knew she'd lost …she'd been too greedy"), there is no warning against this kind of activity. She realises that her trick should have been more subtle; then it would have worked! The final paragraph assures us that Gillian is forced to pay out, but Tamsin makes *some* profit. "It hadn't been a wasted exercise", she says. So where is the moral?

B5) How is deception portrayed in junior fiction?

5.1) Is lying justified?

"The Lord detests lying lips but delights in men who are truthful". (Prov.12:22).

Authors well understand a child's reasons for lying. However, in their attempt to portray this temptation sympathetically, they often only succeed in reinforcing wrong motives. The common euphemism for a lie is "a fib", implying a lesser sin!

In *The Dead Letter Box*, Jan Mark's heroine thinks it reasonable to lie about something she *hopes* is, or will be, true. Louie boasts that she has a terrific idea, when as yet she has none. This attitude has the effect of exchanging truth for intention! More excuses come from Ariadne who lies about her age in *Here Comes Charlie Moon* (by Shirley Hughes). She tells Charlie, "I pretended I was older than I was".

In the past, literary heroes would have taken the honourable path. They would have striven to avoid falsehood at all costs; it was not in their character to resort to a lowering of standards. Indeed authors would not have *led* their heroes into situations which required dishonesty as the only solution. So why do today's writers persuade youngsters that in certain circumstances lying is justified or even necessary when desperate?

After the invocation of the *Greenwitch*, Captain Toms has to lie about the lifeless painter in order to avoid awkward questions. To enquirers, he says that the man must have been hit by a car. For the same reason, Owen Owens explains the noise in his bedroom by telling his mother he dropped a book, when in fact *Tatty Apple* had caused the bed to levitate!

Motivated by self-preservation, the reluctant Father Christmas, Cyril Bonhamy (*Cyril Bonhamy v. Madame Big* by J. Gathorne-Hardy) removes the signpost to his grotto and settles down to a good read. When asked who has taken the notice, he says, "I haven't the faintest idea". This is cowardly deceit.

More complicated is the plight of Suzie, in *Liar, Liar, Pants on Fire* (by Jeremy Strong), who concocts face-saving stories when her dad walks out on the family, possibly even lying to herself to suppress the hurting. It becomes a chronic habit which she cannot stop. When her teacher discovers the truth, her sympathy has the effect of excusing the deception and presenting it as one way of coping with such a betrayal. Even though Suzie is criticised by her friends for her lying, no alternative solution is offered.

The most disturbing quote comes from Margaret Mahy's *The Haunting* in which Tabitha admits, "I always say what's true …It's one of those things that's wrong with me". Her sister who possesses special powers answers, "Better to be like me and tell only lies".

One suspects that even when an apology is forthcoming, it is due to the fact that no further deception is viable! In *T.R.'s Hallowe'en* by T. Dicks, Jimmy assures his mother that his trick-or-treating venture was just fine, even though he had met trouble. When the police arrive he "regrets" his lie and owns up.

5.2) Is dishonesty allowed to go unchallenged?

Some stories focus on dishonesty as a central theme. Deception does not always involve telling lies, but the one is often born out of the other. Take the story of *William and the Mouse* by M. Poulton, from the Oxford Reading Scheme. William allows his pet mouse to run free in the lounge, against his mother's wishes, whist she is out. He ransacks the room trying to find it again. He decides to lure the mouse with food, but is caught at the fridge with the cheese in his hands. "I just wanted to look at it," he lies to his sister. Neither the lies nor the deceit are challenged; what happens when mum returns to the mess is not described. The impression is given that William had no other choice.

Naughty Natalie and the Yellow Paint by J. Lampert is the story of a discontented girl who envies her blond and blue-eyed friends. Whilst her parents are outside, she tiptoes to the paint cupboard and proceeds, with inevitable disaster, to daub her hair bright yellow. It is clear by her furtive manner that she is engaged in deceit; she knows her parents would not approve.

A miniature witch appears and harangues Natalie for being so stupid, and for making a mess, but not for being deceitful! Needing to practise her spells, she offers to magically clear away the evidence and save the girl from trouble. The need for confession and apology is removed! The witch is praised for her brilliance (and collaboration?) and Natalie's secret is safe.

5.3) Are children encouraged into secretive behaviour which is really deceit?

Children enjoy secrets especially when associated with surprises, anticipating the pleasure that will be given or received when the waiting is over. Another kind of secret is that fantasy world that a child inhabits with imaginary friends. This will be explored in a later chapter.

However, there is a sinister aspect to secrecy which is encroaching on youngsters' experience now. It is intermingled with deception and alienation from parents, which has New Age roots. We also see it in cases of abuse when a child has been frightened into keeping facts hidden. It is important for teachers and parents to clarify the issue and encourage trust and openness again within the family.

It is because of the secretive nature of Rose's calling as a Messenger of Favour, in *Cry of a Seagull*, that she finds herself in danger and driven to telling lies as she sets out in Ben's boat to save the donkey. "She had got to do it all alone and no-one must ever know". The incident bears a number of subtle messages to the reader: Don't ask questions; surrender your discernment; allow yourself to be carried along by circumstances. Is this wise advice?

Charlie Dragon by Molly Bond is a book for younger readers. A dragon jumps into George's pocket during a visit to the Fairy Grotto. He decides not to mention his new pet, fearing his parents would forbid him to keep it. This is deceitful behaviour, but more alarming is the assurance that it *is* safe to have friends your parents disapprove of.

Some stories persuade readers that it is *considerate* to hide facts from parents because the truth would worry them! Examples are found in *Rob's Place* and also *The Ghost-Eye Tree* by Martin and Archambault. Why perpetuate secrets for their own sake at the risk of spoiling relationships? It is role-reversal that persuades children to take on a responsibility that should be shouldered by the parents.

5.4) Are craftiness and deceit admired or even rewarded?

In *Dragon Paths*, Tomi accepts the task of guiding some travellers to a distant land, though he knows neither the location nor the language. He is persuaded: "You might have to lie a little bit but it won't be anything serious", but "There's no need to be sickeningly honest", and later, "If you have to lie do it thoroughly"! Tomi feels guilty about the way he has deceived his companions and feels he must make amends – but takes no action! The result of his dishonesty is to gain power, esteem, wealth and a father!

James and the T.V. Star by Michael Hardcastle is one of the Bear Cub series. The cover blurb describes it as a read alone book about "James' good idea … for first solo reading, ideal for building confidence". Would that mean confidence in deceit? James who can be no more than seven years old, is envious of Pippa who has met his T.V. idol, Terry the naturalist "in the flesh". He decides that to go and watch him filming, he will have to abscond from school during the lunch hour when no-one is looking. "He knew he'd have to be brave … to go there on his own", on the bus. This gives a new meaning to bravery, doesn't it?

James steals some beans from the fridge to take for Terry's sickly tortoise. After being motivated by envy, hero-worship and self-will, does James encounter disaster? Certainly not! He meets the star, saves the tortoise's life with the tempting food and appears on T.V. He succeeds in one-upmanship over Pippa and everyone else!

5.5) What guidance is given regarding a) respect of property and b) stealing?

We have seen how deception can lead to other sins. Though well motivated with concern for the tortoise, James had to steal because of the circumstances he had brought on himself. Sadly, stealing occurs in children's books for less worthy ideals, yet often appears to be justified. Big John Turkle has to steal the cup-handle to teach Grover Crow a lesson (*Ponders*)! Tatty Apple may be so clever, but his weakness for chocolates causes him to run off with a box from the shop. His owner Owen Owens is chased but does not apologise. Again, in *Dragon Paths*, Yumi is justified for being sly and thieving because he is a poor cripple. He criticises a fellow thief who was too confident and careless, and so was caught.

Other authors need no excuses. Stealing is the normal way of life for The Fraggles in J.Stevenson's *Red and the Pumpkins*. They live on a staple diet of radishes which only grow in the giant's garden. Keith, of *Rob's Place*, "acquires" a racing-car track. He says, "I didn't ask any questions … Fell off the back of a truck I reckon". Flip, in *Key to the Other*, seizes a bicycle in order to follow the magic door. His psychic friend advises him to keep quiet about it when the bike is lost.

In the *Tim and Tobias* series, the hero under the influence of the magic cat deceives his aunt and sneaks food into his room. Confusing messages are given: in book A3, Captain Jory admits he would be imprisoned if the police could see him, yet in A4 his smugglers explain away the robbing of provisions from the local shop: "You can call it stealing if you like but I don't …We have our way of paying for things". By this they mean that Tobias fixes it for the shopkeeper's wife to win the top prize at bingo! This is really stealing twice over, but the author gives no such clarity, and Tim is easily persuaded to become an accomplice in the conspiracy. There is no question of detection since Tim becomes invisible in the policeman's torch-light.

No wonder the indecisive hero of *Then Again Maybe I Won't* (by J. Blume) is confused. Tony wonders if his friend's shoplifting is any worse than cheating at maths. He accuses his psychiatrist of never giving any answers! Should he report Joel? For fear of losing a friendship he keeps quiet.

What a relief to find a story which makes a very clear statement about the rights of ownership. In *Finders Keepers*, a Young Puffin book by June Crebbin, the heroine is rewarded for returning a stray rabbit. The point is firmly made that finding does *not* mean keeping.

B6) What is the motivating factor?

6.1) What attitudes are rewarded?

A Dog For Ben, a Picture Puffin Book by J.Richardson, tells of a boy who longs for an exciting canine playmate and plans to buy him a studded collar, a chain and lead. To his dismay, he is asked to care instead for an elderly neighbour's lap-dog – a mere bundle of fluff. Ben's reaction is bad tempered and rude, but he eventually becomes fond of the pet and keeps it. This book has a "satisfactory" ending because Ben is happy after all.

This situation is fairly typical of many families today in which the household revolves around the children, trying to maintain the peace by keeping them happy. Happiness is everything: the child's wishes are of paramount importance; the child reigns! This orientation fosters selfishness and produces self-centred adults. The ideology is humanism: "…This is the only life we have so we must strive to make it as happy as possible".

As *Seas of Blood* reveals, the pursuit of wealth, together with a craving for power, often involves aggression as a tool to achieve success. Indeed, aggression itself can be the motivator, as we will see in chapter 8.

In the *Longman Reading Scheme*, there is a story called *The Bracelet*. Kamala endeavours to curb injustice, yet with the help of her magic bangle she scares a child into apologising for being nasty. Is it right to use aggression to induce fear as a control even when the goal is honourable? Does the end justify the means?

In *Tipper Wood's Revenge*, the hero's motivation is obvious from the title, no matter if it does bring a brush with the police. For younger children, Dahl's *Matilda* seeks revenge on her parents who treat her as "nothing more than a scab". She puts super-glue in her father's hat, and when he tears her book in fury, she plans another "suitable punishment for a poisonous parent".

Conrad, the Factory-made Boy is advised by Mrs Bertolotti: "If you don't know what to do ...listen to your own heart". The value of that depends, of course, on its focus and motivation. Christianity teaches that the problems of the world are caused by the sinful nature of the heart. Some, like Louie in *Dead Letter-Box*, are moved to action by omen and co-incidence – the lucky number 7 on her bus ticket tallies with the return date on her library book. Are we encouraging this scratch-card generation to place their hopes on the lucky break? We promote the something-for-nothing mentality when the "happy ending" portrays wish-fulfilment on the material level, brought about by pure chance as in *James and the Giant Peach* (R.Dahl). Through no effort of his own, the poor friendless boy becomes rich and successful with no growth of character and of no benefit to others.

For the humanist who sees no need for life to have an ultimate purpose, there is no point in storing up treasures in heaven by the way we live on earth. Alternatively, religious beliefs greatly affect our philosophy of life and our behaviour in this world.

Adherents of some religions abhor the weakness associated with "losing face". Insecurity produces a fear of ridicule and of being proved wrong. Truth is considered of less importance than the *effect* of one's words on the listener. Pride is regarded as strength; humility, apology and repentance are uncharacteristic. There is strong motivation to maintain one's honour – a word with more than one interpretation! If that honour, or glory, is thought to be threatened, then revenge must be sought. This is the antithesis of Christian values like mercy and forgiveness.

No wonder the gospel of Jesus was thought to be foolishness to the Gentiles (1Cor.1:23). He came as a suffering servant, laying down his life in every way, even for those who ignored him, preaching the security of the Father's love and freedom of guilt through repentance. One senses now the opposing spirits subtly targeting children through their reading.

However, I am sure that you will want your children to be inspired by heroes who are worthy models with admirable goals, or at least to be deterred by the obvious pitfalls of wrong-doing. If only we might see more striving for good and more concern for others in junior fiction. *Me, Jill Robinson and the Stepping Stones Mystery* is an excellent example of youngsters engaged upon a project of benefit to the whole community, rather than themselves. The mystery evolves around their building of a bridge to ease accessibility to a beauty-spot. This book teaches the lesson that the seemingly weak and victimised, in this case the underestimated kid-brother, is often the true hero.

Look out for stories like this in which right attitudes are rewarded. Examples include *All Because of Polly* by Wendy Douthwaite, in which a handicapped girl walks again after attempting to help her friend. The hero of Anne Holm's *I Am David* knows he is forgiven when he finally learns to forgive others. We must encourage our children to create "public demand" for those writers who weave wholesome values into their novels and whose heroes prove to be overcomers, so that our young people may yearn again for excellence and be dissatisfied with anything less.

More Recommended Books

For Younger Readers

Dogger   by Shirley Hughes.

The Giving Tree by S. Silverstein.

 Postman Pat by J.Cunliffe.

Ship's Cook Ginger by Ardizzione.

Katie Morag by M. Hedderwick.

The Night the Animals Fought by J.Zaton.

The Market Square Dog   by J. Heriot.

Bathwater's Hot by Shirley Hughes.

Tim's Last Voyage   by Ardizzone.

One-Eyed Jake by P. Hutchins.

<u>For Older Readers</u>

River's Revenge by J.Collins.

The Latchkey Children by E.Allen.

Jeffey, the Burglar's Cat by Ursula Moray Williams.

Why the Whales Came by M.Morpurgo.

Chapter 6: PERSONAL RELATIONSHIPS

"If we live in the light … we will have fellowship with one another". (1John 1:7)

Jesus was the perfect example of love for God and for others. As the nun explains, in *Nothing Else Matters*, we show our love to God through our acceptance of his ways. It is in the family that we have the opportunity to work out how best to relate with each other through love and respect.

The concept of the traditional family unit is not merely a relic of a previous era; nor is it one of many possible groupings which just happened to be adopted by western society. It has in fact been instigated by God in his wisdom as a place of security, and is also a training ground for good relationships in society. It is an ideal environment in which to serve those who may be older, younger, sick, awkward or ungrateful, whatever one's circumstances. As we search children's literature for messages about personal relationships we must begin with the family.

B7) Does the book make it clear that a stable family unit is the ideal?

7.1) Are the parents shown to be loving, wise and a safe refuge?

"…love which binds all things together in perfect unity". (Col.3:14)

If only there were more examples in fiction of parents keen to build close family relationships. Yes there are some, like *A Gift From Winklesea*, providing positive images of a stable family life. The children, who are lively but obedient, are given wise guidance from their parents. Their sea-side "pebble" hatches out a sort of Loch Ness monster which they keep as a pet until it is too big to handle. No secrecy here; the parents are included in this fantasy of suspense and humour, which brings out caring attitudes and common sense as well as ecological solutions!

More often, we see selfishness and strife. There is disregard for the feelings of others, with only loosely reined aggression surfacing as rudeness. *The Finding* gives the *impression* of a caring family who rescue Alex from abandonment on The Embankment, but turmoil is not far under the surface. Laura tells Alex, "Gran doesn't like Mum sometimes. She looks for ways to upset her … Mum bosses Gran about … and Gran likes to get her own back". Alex feels uncomfortable, suspecting he may be the cause of unrest. Laura assures him, "It isn't your fault. If it wasn't you, they'd find something else to quarrel about". She implies that arguments are a normal pattern of behaviour, in fact she herself enjoys a good quarrel; she finds them exciting.

What pictures of family life are being projected on to the minds of young readers? Are they learning that family life is worthwhile, that its establishment is worth working for though it may take patience and perseverance to succeed; that its strength holds spiritual implication and requires moral application? Are children being taught to honour their parents, to care for and encourage each other?

Thord Cat, hero of *Odin's Monster*, is revered as kind, brave and honest, a man of principle – a good role-model maybe? Far from living happily ever after with his new wife, he says, "Let's stay married until we tire of each other. That will be time enough to part". Diminished expectations result not only in a stubbornly high divorce rate, but also in a mistrust of commitment, with couples preferring merely to "live together".

Latest statistics estimate that 42% of marriages in England and Wales end in divorce. This unstable environment is characterised by stress and difficulty, and often results in children being brought up in an incomplete family unit. The Office for National Statistics records that there are 2 million lone parents with dependant children in the UK, which is 25% of all families with children. It has been found that the effects of the breakdown of the nuclear family are more severe and long-lasting than previously realised. The children of broken homes are more at risk than others, especially when re-marriage occurs and the ensuing conflict may well encourage them to leave home at an early age.

Even so, this *is* still the minority! Unfortunately many writers, in attempting to mirror reality, are presenting this state as the norm and thus perpetuating its acceptability as an alternative option. Some authors even refer to the single parent without it having any bearing on the plot, as though it were a magic ingredient necessary for credibility. The message received confirms that fathers/mothers *are* dispensable. Any variation on the theme is as good as another!

This attitude arises out of the secular need to find one's worth in success. Failure is embarrassing. Children's books follow the current trend to cover up, to avoid losing face; the broken family is bolstered up as adequate. Where is the writer who will present the one parent family truthfully, as deficient of a vital element, yet representing a challenge? A fictional hero who is ready to meet such difficulties and make the best of his circumstances with courage and perseverance would be a great inspiration to a reader with similar problems. The child is still blameless but, as an overcomer, more worthy of admiration.

We almost glimpse such a hero in Townsend's Rob, who longs for his parents to be reconciled. His father's impending re-marriage is seen as the final step in the break-down of his original family. Rob is expected to let go of the old life and accept the new. However, his response to this challenge is to block out reality by creating a fantasy world in which to hide. The only way to handle a difficulty, it seems, is to opt out.

Neither does *Liar, Liar, Pants on Fire* offer any positive way of coping for children of split families. Suzie's mother bitterly asserts that she is glad her husband has left. "He ran off with some cow and good riddance to him. Got some peace and quiet now … and my freedom". The rather negative conclusion is emphasised by Suzie's loss of friends in the course of moving house. Although this book is classified as teenage fiction, the print is large and Suzie only ten years old. Readers tend to choose books about their peers. Is this a suitable subject for this age-group? Is the treatment adequate? Who would enjoy such a story?

Of course, many of the problems facing victims of marriage breakdown are the same for those suffering bereavement. A number of classics have featured children who are orphans, like *Heidi* by Johanna Spyri and Montgomery's *Anne of Green Gables*, or who have one or both parents absent as in *The Silver Sword* and *Little Women* by L.M.Alcott. These stories have been successful in portraying peace and fulfilment in the face of adversity, especially when trusting in God for security.

An unmarried mother ("The bastard took off before I could manage to pin him down") features in *Frankie's Dad*. Rather than faith, we catch a note of hysteria as she cries, "God help me, poor fool that I am!" At her wits end, trying to cope with wayward daughter Frankie, she threatens, "I wish to God that I'd put you into a home. I didn't have to keep you, you know … Nothing but insolence and ingratitude!"

She resorts to marriage as the only way to secure her future, but sees Frankie as the trouble-maker in the new relationship. Is it for selfish reasons that she deliberately closes her eyes to the violence of her new husband towards his son Jass? Frankie's dream of her real dad as a rescuing prince ends in disillusionment, as she realises he is an irresponsible gambler. They are caught in a net of hopelessness which affects the reader too. We sense no real change of attitude even in the eventual truce between mother and daughter.

After encountering both Frankie's dad and her step-father, a reader might agree with self-sufficient Mrs. Bartolotti (in *Conrad, the Factory-Made Boy*) who does not believe it is absolutely necessary for a seven-year-old boy to have a father. In *this* story, Conrad has to teach his unconventional parent how to behave. However, it is the roles of mother and father that are more likely to be reversed today, a fact that is reflected in young fiction.

7.2) Does the father match up to the Christian model of fatherhood?

The Bible tells us that man was made in the image of God, whom we are to call Father. It follows then that earthly fathers have been so named after their heavenly example, with potential to emulate His qualities and to receive respect from the family (Ephesians 3:14). It is expected that they will shoulder responsibility in the family in a caring way, just as Christ is the head of the church, says St. Paul ((Eph.5:23).

Unfortunately, the strong decisive father figure, such as we find in *Nick and the Glimmung*, has become a victim of women's liberation and ignored in fiction. Rather than the symbol of protection portrayed by Nick's father, readers are being conditioned to accept the small, weak Cyril Bonhamy type, nervous of his tall domineering wife as she chooses a job for him from the "Sits. Vac." column. There are many examples. Roderick Hunt's *The Ice Giants*, (one of the Oxford Reading Tree titles) sports a picture of Dad in the garden, supposedly mowing the lawn, but actually lazing on a sun-bed with not one but *four* cans of beer!

In their attempt to reach the modern child, authors have so reacted against stereotyping that they have swung too far in the opposite direction. With women's emancipation has come the emasculation of fathers, both of which tend to be exaggerated. Is this a writers' campaign against fathers or merely a reflection of how things are? Even if stress and its escape routes are a regrettable reality, is there any need to inflict these models on our children?

Roald Dahl often features objectionable adults in his works. *Matilda* must surely have the most hateful parents of all, vulgar, unloving and dishonest. Her mother says of her skinny husband that he is "hardly the kind of man a wife dreams about". More subtle though is the deception sown in his *Danny, the Champion of the World*, a book described by *The Listener* as "a delightfully acute portrayal of the relationship between a growing boy and his widowed father". How innocent that sounds!

The first three chapters build up a picture of the perfect dad, loving, wise, inventive and great fun to be with. In the fourth chapter the reader is told that all parents have two or three hidden vices. Then it is revealed that William considers himself above the law. He has kept Danny away from school for two years, asserting that *he* knows best. He is also crazy about poaching pheasants! He denies it is stealing, preferring to call it an art. He proceeds to teach Danny the skills of this exciting nocturnal activity, giving it a respectability akin to hunting, and winning approval from the vicar and the doctor! For William, the danger of being caught is "the biggest thrill of all". Is this responsible behaviour?

Just as regrettable is the father who has no time to talk or play with his children. Though one suspects a message more to the parent than to the child, the point is well-made in *My Dad Doesn't Even Notice* by Mike Dickinson. The title is used as a refrain on every page. To take one example, Dad arrives home late complaining he has been held up in the traffic. He is too tired to realise that he is also being held up in the hall by his son dressed as a cow-boy, and wishing that dad would use more imagination!

A similar point is made in A.Baillie's *Adrift* for older children. The father always has his back turned, "the head hunched under a desk lamp". To a young reader, the sense of joining ranks with others who suffer the same neglect may have the effect of deepening resentment against the offending parent.

7.3) Is the mother true to the feminine role?

Whilst God created Eve as a support and complement to Adam, Isaiah speaks of mothers as comforters to their children (Is.66:13). The classic reference to the role of women in Proverbs 31 calls her to watch over the affairs of her household, to be wise and busy. Her family will praise her, for she is "worth more than rubies" (v.10 & 28). Although St. Paul directs wives to submit to their husbands, this is not an attitude of subjection. There is dignity in this obedience. Respect must be mutual (Col.3:18,19). Eve's was a high calling: to be mother of all the living (Gen.3:20). There is no question of inferiority here. Throughout Scripture there emerges a picture of womankind as sensitive helpers and carers whose feminine qualities are of great value to the family.

The abdication of men from their rightful place in the family has left the way open for the mother to be dominant. The epitome of the Amazonian mother appears in Ivor Cutler's *Meal One*. She plays football and wrestles on the floor with son Helbert, though in the illustration he looks as though he would like to throttle her! It is obvious she idolises him, for the picture of her kneeling before Helbert to dress him suggests an attitude of worship. "My beautiful son!" she croons, and carries him to breakfast. There is no father in evidence.

Unlike Lamia's mother in *Nothing Else Matters*, who is appreciated by her husband as "his rock in the storm, his peace", *Rags and Riches* (by Joan Lingard) offers Isabella as the modern mother giving Seb and Sam free rein. Here is the liberal face of humanism which says, "Do what you like!" However she is rather immature and impulsive: her inconsistency gives no security.

As well as the easy-going mother-figure, which would make some youngsters feel dissatisfied with their own lot, we also find more negative images occurring. In *Ghost-Eye Tree*, Mama seems not to understand her children's fear of the dark. She tells them to fetch some milk from the other end of town, "one dark and windy autumn night when the sun had long gone down". Does she not care that they are terrified? "Oooo I dreaded to go", cries the little one. Can they not *tell* her they are scared of the ghostly tree?

The Dead Letter Box portrays a mother insensitive to her daughter's feelings, who even disapproves of her reading books! These various expressions of motherhood are in complete contrast with the gentle feminine attributes which reflect the compassionate nature of God.

7.4) How do the siblings relate to one another?

Turning to other relationships within the family, let us examine that between brothers and sisters. Rivalry between siblings is normal, but calls for self-control and a positive attitude if harmony is to prevail. Writers who address this problem seem to stress the differences, often for the sake of humour, but fall short on the solutions! One would expect Gary to be grateful when *The Red and White Scarf* (by Roderick Hunt), painstakingly knitted by his sister, saves him from falling down a cliff, but there is no sign of appreciation at all. Blume's *The Pain and the Great One* contrasts the brother's and sister's opinions of one another. Though there is the assurance that both are loved by their parents, there is no meeting half-way for the rivals.

Catherine Storr chooses the close bond between twins for her theme in *Puss and Cat*. Seeking for their own identities, the sisters decide to take separate adventure holidays, likewise their brother Tom. Having wandered off along a lonely beach, Puss discovers Tom in danger. He has broken his leg, is unable to move, and the tide is advancing! Puss struggles to move him up the beach, inch by inch, willing Cat to come to her aid. On the face of it, a good message: when in trouble, twins need each other. However there is a strong suggestion of the use of telepathy.

Whilst Richard Graham portrays Jack's baby brother as a monster in *Jack and the Monster,* Shirley Hughes' *The Trouble with Jonathan* highlights the nuisance of a kid brother. The best that can be achieved is sisterly tolerance. Jan Ormerod is far more helpful. She offers *101 Things to Do With a Baby* as a therapy for older siblings. This lively picture-book turns the chore of caring for a toddler into an exciting family pastime! In the first picture, mother is discreetly breast-feeding the baby whilst cuddling the older child under the other arm —a message here for mothers!

B8) How do fictional children relate to their elders?

8.1) Do the children respect their parents?

Obviously, if there is conflict between parents, it will be caught by the other members of the family. Literature tends to highlight antagonism between the generations. In the very first line of *Crummy Mummy and Me* by Anne Fine, the child complains, "I don't think my mum's fit to be a parent". It had to come, a story featuring punk parents!

Even for more conventional types, there is lack of respect from their offspring. Sam, who is one of the *Friends at Pine Street* (by M.E. Allen), orders her father to take her to the museum. "I've got to have another look 'cos I have an idea". Mr. Padgett "agreed meekly". It is a fact that the contempt felt for parents has arisen out of the lack of adequate boundaries of behaviour, reinforced by fictional examples which tell the reader, "This is how you speak to parents".

Children must obey their parents, but first they need to know what the rules are! The Bible teaches that parents must train their children to live in a way that pleases God (Eph.6:1-4), for whoever truly loves his son is careful to discipline him (Prov.13:24; 22:6). This makes sense of the command to love your father and mother. It is clear that these guidelines are for our good, and for a peaceful and orderly life.

From their reading books, youngsters are being taught alternative strategies. Abigail, of *It's Abigail Again* (by Moira Miller), though lovable, is a naughty and strong-willed five-year-old. She is disciplined more by coaxing and humouring than by any firm hand. In contrast, *Voices* gives the warning that Julia is in bondage to her mother's ways, ever conscious of what she would say, even when separated.

There are many instances of children taking action without parental consent and especially of going out alone. A couple of examples will suffice here. *Paul, Sally and Little Grey* by Harry Iseborg is at first glance a happy little story for 6-7 year-olds about nature, about helping each other and with a moral about a thieving magpie thrown in for good measure. However, Paul and Sally go off into the woods and stay out all day without even a word to their parents!

Sheila McCullagh was and still is a well-known name for beginner reading schemes, one of her most popular being *One, Two, Three and Away* (readily available on-line). But watch out for the characters who slip away alone to the woods at night, like Jennifer Yellow-Hat in *The Cat's Dance (Bk.5)* and Melanie in *The Horse That Flew in the Moonlight (Yellow Bk.10)*.

In the case of *Tipper Wood's Revenge, Frankie's Dad,* and *Liar, Liar, Pants on Fire,* we see youngsters who are little more than an inconvenience to their single parents' search for personal fulfilment. Frankie and Jass are left at a loose end while their parents honeymoon. Tipper fends for himself while Dad is on holiday. As long as they have enough money, they can cope, thus fuelling the resentment against parental control.

In complete contrast we find the security of discipline the underlying theme of Maurice Sendak's *Where the Wild Things Are*. Those who criticise this book for its scary pictures have missed the real point. Because Max has been behaving so badly, his mum calls him "a wild thing" and sends him to bed. His room becomes a fantasy world where wild beasts live. Max learns that he can take authority over these monsters and resist them. He also realises that he prefers the safety of his home where he is loved by caring parents.

Children appreciate parents who are responsible. They lose confidence in those who opt out, with the resultant breakdown of communication between the generations. As we saw in chapter 5, the child's love of secrets is being exploited in literature by promoting the misconception that some things cannot be shared with adults because they would not understand. In Betsy Byars' *The Cartoonist*, Alfie lies about what he does in the attic as a defence against his family's prying. Clearly a distinction must be made between secrecy and privacy, and the difference explained to children.

Is there a hint of a conspiracy to alienate parents and present them as "the enemy"? Perhaps the sceptic may be convinced that this is not an exaggerated view if we consider for a moment the United Nations' Children's Charter. This international treaty was drawn up in 1989 with the aim of "protecting children". But reading between the lines, we find that there is a tendency to restrict parental influence and discipline, particularly of a religious nature, in favour of the children's rights to do as they please. Anything which conflicts with the God-given role of parenthood needs careful scrutiny.

8.2) Do we see models for right attitudes to older people, e.g. grandparents?

Leila Berg's *Little Pete* can be no more than five years old, yet his attitude to adults is exceedingly cheeky. When loudly reprimanded by a neighbour for pulling plants out of his garden, Pete retorts, "You shouldn't shout". The impression given is that Pete is wiser than the grown-ups around him, and that he has every right to scold them. He accuses one, "You should help me. You know that don't you?" and to another, "You are silly". It is not until chapter 8 that anyone cautions Pete about his manners.

An old lady is treated with derision in Shirley Hughes' *It's Too Frightening For Me.* When two young boys break into her old house, Granny discovers them with such a shock that she cries, "AAAAUGH , gobble, gobble, gob − get out, GET OUT", whereupon her grand-daughter tells her to behave herself! She is made to look ridiculous. There is also a worrying tendency to refer to old women as witches, as in *Tipper Wood's Revenge* and *T.R.Bear's Hallowe'en*, or as "old bats" as in Sheila Lavelle's *The Boggy Bay Marathon.*

I once had the opportunity to question a 10-year-old about his school library book, *George's Marvellous Medicine* by Roald Dahl. He told me:

"It's about a lazy grandmother".

"Do you think *real* grandmothers are lazy?"

"Some are".

"Oh! Do you know any?"

 "Yes, my Mum's mother"

I used the occasion to speak to him about grandmothers needing time to sit and rest in their old age because they tire easily and often suffer from aches and pains. I assured him that his grandma would have worked very hard when she was fitter. Unfortunately he went on to read *The Finding* which will have reinforced the negative images.

For a positive message, choose *Katie Morag Delivers the Mail* by Mairi Hedderwick. Here more realistically we see an active grannie who drives a tractor and helps Katie out of a crisis.

B9) Is the reader given a positive view of authority?

"…The authorities that exist have been established by God…" (Romans 13:1)

Messages which undermine respect for what used to be called one's elders and betters are infiltrating even picture-books. School is an environment where authority is structured to various levels so that harmony and order facilitate education. Imagine school lunches without supervision, yet the hero of *Dinner Ladies Don't Count* (listed as Key Stage 1) takes little notice of Mrs Moors till she threatens to kill him! This reaction, imposed by the author, does little to improve the image or further the cause of lunch-time supervisors.

Humphrey Carpenter not only gives dinner ladies and their cooking some bad publicity in *Mr Majeika and the Dinner Lady*, but also causes the pupils to be rude about a school governor. Because she is upset about bad behaviour, they call her "an old cow" and "the silly old bag … with a face like a bent bicycle wheel".

As may be expected, school staff occur frequently in junior fiction, but are rarely shown in a favourable light. In *The Witch V.I.P.*, Simon comments on the new head-teacher: "It is very tiresome to start getting used to another rotten head", and then, "He'd never actually seen Mr Bodley doing any work".

A similar observation about the teacher in *Enough Is Enough* by Margaret Nash has no relevance to the story. Further personal remarks about the large hole in her tights are also quite unnecessary, except for the purpose of ridicule. This small volume contains a strange mixture of three separate stories. The first is complete fantasy, whereas the others are supposed to be true to life. The class are particularly boisterous, chewing gum and throwing apple cores. Is this the best example to give to impressionable youngsters who are just beginning to Read Alone, for that is the purpose of this Series.

Lack of respect leads to lack of trust and gives rise to feelings of insecurity. Suspicion is sown by false information. Dahl goes to great lengths to explain, in *The Witches*, that "your teacher" may be a witch if she has large "nose-holes" and wears a wig. The fear is greater because the writer has set up the grandmother as an authority on the subject and emphasises that what she says is "gospel truth". Surely children should not be confused about such things?

Maybe the lack of confidence in authority figures fuels the defiance that is present in fiction and in reality. When Puss the twin (*Puss and Cat*) returns very late to the camp with Tom and his broken leg, she is severely reprimanded for straying from the coach-party and causing worry and inconvenience. "It wasn't my fault. It was yours!" she accuses the group-leader. She is unrepentant, even proud of her heroism. It is implied that her thoughtless, self-willed actions are justified because Tom has been rescued. No doubt Puss would support Sam, one of the *Friends at Pine Street* who asserts, "Rules can be broken if they're stupid!"

Suspicion is evident too with regard to the police. The *Witch V.I.P.* hints that the police are failing in their duty by passing the time playing cards. Tipper Wood and his mates take detective work into their own hands because the police do not appear interested. These messages invite anti-authority attitudes.

Without people's acceptance of authority, orderly society breaks down and becomes anarchy. St. Paul tells us to show respect and pray for our leaders so that all may live peaceably (1Tim.2:1-3). This is somewhat surprising when we consider the Roman occupation of Palestine and other lands in those days and the hardships imposed. Yet Jesus led no revolt against the army, the government or even tax-collectors! He blessed the Roman centurian who himself was "a man under authority" and wisely recognised its benefits. Even under harsh regimes God has worked powerfully to bring good out of evil through the Christ-like attitudes of Christian believers.

One may regard the odd reference to a councillor as "a geezer" (in *Dog Powder*), or to the head of the army as a "silly man" (*The B.F.G.*), as too insignificant to campaign about. However, when viewed as part of the whole literary scene one realises that the many disparaging remarks fit together like the pieces of a large jigsaw puzzle in the receptive mind of the child. What picture is being assembled? What is the vision for society in future? If children are encouraged to respect others, they will find self-respect and become more responsible citizens.

B10) Are children learning how to relate to their peers?

10.1) Are children being taught to be prejudiced against minorities?

Rather than helpful models, we find conflict characterised either by aggression or loneliness. *The Dead Letter Box* highlights poor Louie's admiration for the extrovert Glenda who really is no chum at all. Catherine Sefton's *Island of the Strangers*, set in Ireland, portrays Nora as having no comfortable relationships with any of the other characters. Even her friend Orla walks off without a word, leaving her on the island in the late evening. Here too we see the power of the bully, Brendan, whose influence over Nora is stronger than her allegiance to her guardian.

Blubber is written from the bully's perspective. Though not the ring-leader, Jill *is* one of the gang who terrorise the fat girl. There seems to be a lesson here for survival in the classroom jungle: those who suffer bullying must have deserved it! There is no retribution for the gang, but Jill learns that if you ally yourself with a bully, that bully may turn on you. She seeks refuge in a new friend, but there is no hope for Blubber.

We see assertive girls protecting weak boys. In *Conrad, the Factory-Made Boy*, the hero is persecuted at school for being so good, but refuses to fight back. Kitty comes to his rescue. She "drove one fist into Frank's stomach, bashed him on the head …and kicked his shins", to the approval of Mrs Bertolotti.

It seems that anyone singled out as different from the majority is vulnerable to prejudice. One such section of society is the handicapped. We see examples of derision in *Voices* when Win sings about poor little Willie who "is deaf, dumb, lame and insane", and also in *Frankie's Dad* with its reference to a "nut-house". How refreshing to read of the courage of wheelchair-bound Beckie who saves her caring friend from an accident in *All Because of Polly*.

The Spell Singer and Other Stories was specially commissioned and published in association with the National Library for the Handicapped Child. The book's aim − to highlight the problem of living with handicaps and to show how they may be overcome − sounds most laudable, but though some of its stories are good, others raise doubts. In one chapter (*The Tinker's Curse* by Joan Aiken), the heroine who is deaf because of a curse develops a compensatory gift of clairvoyance! The title story by Anna Lewins tells of the dyslexic pupil of a school for witches who *sings* her spells in order to remember them! She develops this theme in *The Key to the Other*, where her blond dyslexic hero holds extraordinary knowledge and power.

One parent in Cardiff found it necessary to write in protest to his daughter's primary school head about *The Friends* by Rosa Guy. The girl had chosen it to take home as part of the new book-reading initiative in the school. As well as complaining about the slang, pidgin English, Americanisms, blasphemy and plainly crude language, the father was concerned about racism which he felt was dealt with in "a bald manner", such that would cause fear in primary school children. He felt sure the staff could not be acquainted with the offensive exchanges between the characters, such as:-

"You dirty West Indian …you ain't rapping so big out here, is you?"

"We ain't got us trees to swing from."

"Yeah, she gonna smash that monkey into a African monkey stew."

Racism will be further explored in chapter 7, but in the area of peer-group relationships several questions arise. When considering unsatisfactory friendship models, one must ask whether the inadequacy is exposed, or is normality implied? How do our heroes cope with their needs for acceptance and their developing independence? Are readers left with negative feelings of insecurity and suspicion, or are they inspired to overcome differences and develop good relationships? Do stories incorporate attitudes of kindness, generosity or thoughtfulness of others' needs, not in a sentimental way but in a contemporary package acceptable to modern readers?

10.2) What messages are being given regarding boy/girl relationships and sexual morality?

Remember the *Nancy Drew Mysteries*? In 1986, publishers Simon and Shuster announced she was to be rejuvenated! The old Nancy was dead; she was to be given a sexier, more titillating image. In *Grange Hill Rebels* (by Redmond and Angus) children can read about a pupil's affair with a teacher, whilst books for older juveniles feature incest, irresponsible pregnancy, abortion, lesbianism and homosexuality. The years of carefree innocence have been invaded.

Everyone Else's Parents Said Yes (by Paula Danziger) is an unedifying collection of pre-adolescent ideas, arguments and actions with a very American flavour. The hero's sister is only thirteen, yet her parents are so proud of her setting off on her first date that they record the occasion on film. It is not only novels from the U.S. which encourage precocious behaviour. Kitty's reward for Conrad for eventually behaving badly is a kiss on the mouth, illustrated by a line drawing. This surely is not natural behaviour for seven-year-olds?

10-11 year-olds, whilst enjoying the fantasy world of *Rob's Place*, are being exposed to sexual innuendoes which will be significant in shaping adolescent morality. In one example, Keith tells Rob, "Helen's the first baby I've had, that I'm aware of". The images will lie dormant in the child's mind, gathering reinforcing material until fully assimilated, that is, unless preventative measures are taken by responsible adults to counteract false teaching.

An Ash-Blond Witch by Kenneth Lillington depicts the blond and blue-eyed Sophie as having such supple curves that the men of Urstwhile fall out with their wives, so deranged are they over her beauty. She is not only a witch but a dominant woman from the 22nd century where marriages are extinct and the terms "divine" and "unseemly" considered archaic. Her aim is to seduce Simon. The pious Prudence is sneeringly described as "a judge of the community's morals ...She disapproved of sex altogether" – and we are still in chapter one!

Are writers exploiting the adolescent's interest in sexual matters to gain readership and air their own liberal theories? One of the most popular authors is Judy Blume. She maintains that her themes are those that youngsters want to know about. I expect she is right! Girls, who are far keener readers than boys, are reaching puberty as young as ten-years-old nowadays. But do *you* want your child taught the facts of life by Ms Blume?

One of her heroes, Tony of *Then Again, Maybe I Won't*, has two overriding though unrelated issues to cope with in his life – his parents coming into money, and his growing sexual curiosity at the age of thirteen. He struggles with his conscience over his habit of watching Lisa through his binoculars from his bedroom window as she undresses. Although his is a church-going family and a moral stance could have been brought in naturally, there is nothing said about self-control. Tony decides that his voyeurism is not a sin since it harms no-one. There is no warning that fuelling sexual desires makes avoidance of temptation more difficult, thus harming oneself. The "laissez-faire" humanist attitude cuts across parents' beliefs and ignores the spiritual dimension.

The stories named so far in this section have been for the middle age-group but we must remember that books for young teens will be found in junior libraries and chosen by any competent readers. In some cases identical copies will also be found in the teenage section. There is almost no limit to the range of sexual topics covered. Booksellers justify their carrying of the notorious *Forever* by claiming that it is clearly classified on their shelves as a teenage book. However, Judy Blume herself has stated that she aimed this book at children of twelve years and upwards. She felt there was a need for a responsible attitude towards sexuality and maintains that the prevailing attitude of her characters is *against* casual sex. However, it appears they are not against a full sexual relationship which is not "forever" between two unmarried teenagers.

For those who promote relativism, moral values are no longer regarded as absolute, fixed by God's standards. Extra-marital sex may be right or wrong they say, according to circumstances. One should be watchful of these trends creeping into otherwise helpful books. Although Voight gives a sympathetic portrayal of the church and writes very sensitively in *Come A Stranger* on matters of race and family relationships, notice the humanist voice occasionally breaking through. Whilst Mina has a high regard for her father's opinions, when asked if she would live with a man without marrying, she replies that it would depend on how much she loved him! This is not the Christian way.

Time Rope by Robert Leeson is one of Longman's "Knockouts", a series intended for "slightly more reluctant readers of 11-16". Double standards are in evidence as Fiona escapes a fate worse than death at the hands of a rough navigator, only to yield willingly later to her rescuer. As the story moves from the past to the future, the violent element merges with the sexual. This kind of material, produced merely to titillate, is not worthy to be called literature.

Whilst publishers such as Longman's can describe a series like *Time Rope*, which features amongst other things patricide, sexual encounters, attempted rape, assault and swearing, as being for readers "…not yet ready for adult fiction", it is impossible to have confidence in their editorial selections. The promotion of such unrestrained attitudes ignores the problems of emotional and spiritual anguish, not to mention the physical harm involved. St. Paul cautioned that he who sins sexually, sins against his own body (Cor.6:18).

Surely we must be striving to raise standards, rather than succumb to the seductive permissiveness which only degrades humanity. It was reported in *The Guardian* that 30% of female rape victims are under 16 and 25% were 14 or younger (Office For National Statistics). These figures have increased over the past twenty years. Children are now being supplied with free contraceptives and morning after pills.

A spokeswoman for the End Violence Against Women Coalition says these alarming statistics must be a wake-up call for every profession working with young people and to all of us. She asks, "What are we going to do about this horrific level of assault against young women and girls?" Diane Abbott M.P., as shadow health minister, said, "The rising numbers of girls having under-age sex is alarming …It poses public health policy challenges and social challenges."

The late Linda Lee-Potter, writing in the Daily Mail in 1990, made a plea to the church to speak out with courage and "stop the rot". She expressed a desire for the church to "set moral standards for people". She spoke out strongly against one-parent families as a cause of much unhappiness and welcomed a return to monogamy and fidelity. As a secular journalist, she revealed a rare spiritual insight as she wrote:

"Look at anybody who lacks any basic morality and you don't see free smiling spirits enjoying a fulfilled life. On the contrary you see dissatisfied, desolate people thrashing around in search of something that will appease a gnawing sense of arid, empty bitterness …Morality isn't restrictive, oppressive or vengeful. It is merely a basic blue-print for a reasonably happy existence based on common sense".

Basic Christian principles make sense. Let us take up the challenge, speak out, take action and stand firm on the word of God which is sharper than a two-edged sword and reaches the very heart of the matter.

More Recommended Books

For Younger Readers

Lucy and Tom's Day   by   S. Hughes.

Peabody.   by R. Wells.

Grandma's Bill   by   M. Waddell.

Friends and Brothers   by   D.K. Smith.

Bet You Can't by   P. Dale.

Mog and Barnaby by   J. Kerr.

Blue Boat   by   Dick Bruna. (deafness)

Borka   by   J. Burningham.

Flat Stanley by   J. Brown.

A Kindle of Kittens by R. Godden.   (adopted child)

Berron's Tooth by   J. Solomon.   (teacher)

Uncle Elephant by A. Lobel.   (elders)

Bod and the Dog by M. Cole. (policeman)

For Older Readers

Rose by   E. Beresford.

Treasures of the Snow by P.S. John.

When Hitler Stole Pink Rabbit by J. Kerr. (Jewish family)

Swan by J. Gardam. (mute Chinese boy)

Me Too by   V. & B. Cleaver. (spotlights autism)

Chinese Puzzle by   H. Graham. (guardian)

Chapter 7: "ISMS", BANDWAGONS, & PROPAGANDA

"understand what the Lord's will is …"   (Ephesians 5:17)

C) Is the book being used as a medium of propaganda?

Propaganda is the systematic dissemination of information regarding a philosophy or practice when its benefits are debatable. The word suggests persuasion by a zealous few wishing to make converts, perhaps by unethical tactics.

Some would regard the young mind as virgin soil ready for planting, or even as clean blotting paper whose raison d'etre is to absorb any fresh idea impressed upon it. Many authors exploit the vulnerability of children. They speak obliquely through their main characters, knowing the young reader will empathise with the heroes as friends and receive their words without question.

How long our children will remain innocent, in the widest sense of the word, is surely the prerogative of their parents to decide. They are individual personalities, maturing at different rates. They need careful handling if they are not to be bruised by the world.

Having been taught about "stranger danger", many youngsters are learning to be cautious. They are becoming aware that some adults may want to deceive them. Of course, there are still those who cannot understand this and are prey to the obvious peril. For young children, the concept of untrustworthy grown-ups is very frightening. To build their confidence, parents and others responsible for their development usually ensure that infants are surrounded only by those whose influence is helpful.

As we accept this principle with regard to physical danger, so we must accept the parallel with reading materials which may lead children down dubious mental or spiritual avenues. Sadly they are rarely made aware of propaganda in literature. One would hope that at the secondary level, pupils might be taught to recognise bias as part of the English curriculum, but for the younger age-group their protection depends on the discernment of parents and teachers.

Any teaching which is contrary to that of the Bible should be questioned, even if it appears to be harmless. God has shown us through his written word, and in Jesus, what is good and true. Therefore all other "good ideas" must be weighed against God's standards.

C1.0) Does the book present personal philosophies, superstition, or folk-lore as truth?

"See that no-one takes you captive through hollow and deceptive philosophy which depends on human tradition … " (Colossians 2:8)

The influence of humanism, of New Age ideas and other religions has already been investigated. Now we turn to a few selected examples from the many available that promote personal philosophies born out of human wisdom. It is often illuminating to read what the cover blurb and the occasional newspaper article has to say about certain authors.

When interviewed by *The Independent*, Alan Garner confided that he has *never* set out to write for children. Coming from an educational background of rationalistic Hellenism, he wished his works to be understood "either as modern day variations on ancient mythological themes, or as spare, unsentimental accounts of late childhood". He insisted that the myths which underlie each volume, e.g. Mabinogion for *The Owl Service,* are "meant to be buried so deeply in the narrative that they will not trouble the unaware reader". Is that sufficient to safe-guard the subconscious?

Of *Elidor*, which according to Wikipedia is a children's fantasy novel, Garner himself said it was the only nihilistic book he had ever written. Nevertheless, *The Moon of Gomrath* reveals some disturbingly negative ideas: "Strange words … burned like fire in his brain, sanctuary in the blackness that filled the world".

It is worth noting that J.R.Townsend was one of those who acclaimed *Elidor* as a success. One suspects Garner's influence over him on reading, in *Golden Journey,* that fate over-rules God. Townsend suggests that when you open your mind by meditation, god comes in. He develops the theme that man, or even woman, may become "the living God". He points out that his ideas are not based on any known religion. Nevertheless, they leave a lasting impression.

They are in fact the reversal of the Christian gospel which reveals that *God* became *Man* in order to die for our sins, the only way that man might become righteous. And it is the human spirit that comes alive with the Spirit of God, resulting in the Christian rebirth, not through meditation, but by repentance and acceptance of forgiveness by God's grace.

Superstition abounds, particularly in stories with ghosts or magical themes, and promotes the idea that protection and good luck go hand in hand. Nicholas Stuart Gray informs us, in *A Wind From Nowhere*, that rowan berries are a shield against witchcraft, whilst *Tim and Tobias (Bk.4)* are told that a lamp brings good luck. The latter supposedly originates with the truth that God's Word is "a lamp to my feet" (Ps.119:105).

Whether Leon Garfield's intention is to scorn or to uphold the beliefs and customs associated with Midsummer's Eve is unclear. However, his power to influence by skilful prose is certain. In the very first paragraph of *The Dumb Cake* a spell is woven:

"…when herbs and brimstone turn in the dish and show their darker side; when milkmaids prepare to shudder in churchyards and bakers' daughters gather their friends to bake the dumb cake and see the phantoms of their lovers chasing them upstairs…"

The apothecary's apprentice, Parrot, is scathing about Betty Martin ("silly cow" is the expression he often uses) who indulges in these remedies and rituals. As a seeker after truth he reflects, "A wise man must always be lonely in a world of fools". Is that true? The Book of Proverbs teaches that by wisdom you "will walk in the ways of good men" (2:20) and will be blessed (3:18)!

Despite Parrot's doubts, the success of the dumb cake and the planting of hemp seeds at midnight provide a fund of instructive ideas for those wishing to dabble in superstition even for fun. "They have been playing with magic without realising the terrible fact of it!" And in *this* story, who is grumbling?

C2.0) Does the book contain unsuitable adult messages?

Garfield's little picture-book of less than fifty pages appears to belong with the 8-9 age-bracket. However, the language is rather obscure at times, and I would suspect some matters to be above readers' heads. A midwife enters the apothecary's shop to buy St.John's Wort and Rue as protection against hobgoblins and to ensure a successful confinement for her client "what is stopped up tighter than a drum". She has already tried "sitting the mother over a bowl of steaming Betony water … to bring her to bed of an heir".

The apothecary uses the same herbs in the hope his wife will conceive a child. He can hardly wait to get into bed. Will the readers understand these things? *Should* they understand? If not, why are they included? One might ask similar questions of the suggestive narrative on the last page, when Betty (whom he hates, doesn't he?) finally pins Parrot down and gives him a love potion. Canoodling is hinted –

"Hemp seeds I've sown. Now the crop's to be mown".

– when Parrot quotes from Revelation 8:1 – "And there was silence in heaven for the space of about 'alf an hour".

Surely Nostlinger is aiming her remarks at adults when, in her story of *Conrad,* Mrs Bertolotti says, "Grown-ups like to trick children into believing things … It makes them feel good and clever". Yet as she transmits her message about the insincerity of parents, her words hold the authority of an adult. Should children believe her and become suspicious and fearful? Surely they would be unable to cope with the suggestion that their elders "put on a face" to hide their insecurity?

John Burningham speaks to adults through his "Shirley" picture-books, ostensibly suitable for the very young. *Come Away From the Water, Shirley* contrasts two scenarios between which there is no communication the real world of the parents on the left-hand page which is only a pale shadow of the colourful fantasy world of their daughter fighting pirates on the right-hand page! What will children make of this? The irony of the situation must be beyond the grasp of those who would choose both this book and *Time to Get Out of the Bath, Shirley*, in which mum admonishes the girl for the state of the bathroom, whilst Shirley jousts with knights, miles away in time and space!

Bernard Ashley speaks *on behalf* of youngsters in *I'm Trying to Tell You* when he highlights their difficulty in communicating with parents and teachers. It is a point that needs to be made − but is this the best vehicle for expressing it? Will it not stir up discontent amongst those who read it, reinforcing a "them and us" mentality?

C3.0) Are children being exposed to political propaganda?

One might suppose that political issues are above the heads of children. Nevertheless, they appear in young fiction in various guises serving as opinion- shapers for developing intellects. We may find the casual remark such as, "Really it is called the Job Centre, but the No-Job Centre is what Brendan Egg calls it and he is right" (in *Island of the Strangers*).We may hear the odd protest about the closure of small schools and the public being powerless to stop it (*Dead Letter Box*), or even the plight of the homeless.

This is Bernard Ashley's theme in *Down and Out*, a simple story most suitable for older backward readers, but there is no mention of this on the cover. William is continually being moved on from one hostel to the next. As he helps the elderly Nellie in her garden, she learns to overcome her suspicion of him. "You don't have to be old to be on the skids, ma'am," he tells her. Are children ready for this? To be made aware that some teenagers are homeless, with no reason given, may well give rise to anxiety. The moral, that one should be a Good Samaritan and give such people a chance, is more suitable for those with the power to help. The fact that William moves on and out of Nellie's life provides a sad, if realistic, ending with political overtones.

Joan Lingard slips her point of view into *Rags and Riches* when Granny's trust in the government knowing what is best for people makes Sam seethe! Michael Palin takes a cynical look, through *Cyril and the House of Commons* (Picture Puffin), at what he regards as the boring futility of M.P.s endlessly discussing the reflation of the economy. The hero is able to change people and places by staring at them! In turning Parliament into an amusement park, he is quite blatantly making a travesty of our political system.

We discovered in the previous chapter that a general distrust of authority is taking hold, beginning in the home and extending as far as the law of the land. When Hogarth and his family are terrified by the *Iron Man* they feel they cannot turn to the police or the army because "nobody would believe them". This is rather an absurd statement considering all the evidence littering the landscape! They take the law into their own hands. Having caught the monster in a pit, they plan to destroy him with anti-tank guns!

This contempt for the Establishment is the same spirit that underlies anarchy. It is misplaced in children's books. It sows seeds of discontent about matters incomprehensible to the young which will surface as a rebellious spirit later on. That is not to say that *adults* should be deterred from independent thought and constructive criticism. They however have the power to work within the system rather than against it. Our politicians may not be perfect, being ordinary mortals who make mistakes, but compared with anarchy our democratic system is by far the most desirable for a free and orderly society. To be viable it needs popular acceptance.

Those with a political axe to grind have been keen to take advantage of literary opportunities. Ironically, and for this very reason, Marxist writer Jack Zipes, addressing an adult readership, (*Breaking the Magic Spell: Radical Theories of Folk and Fairy Tales*), has attempted to expose as harmful the traditional values in fairy tales because he recognises the deep impression they make. Other campaigners produced a whole series of picture-books during The Year of the Child illustrating children's rights.

Andi's War, set in the Greek civil war, has much to say of a political nature. It is worth noting that this story won the Faber/Guardian/Jackanory Children's Writers competition in 1988. In the Foreword of this disturbing book, the author tries to be fair, pointing out that atrocities were committed on both sides. She describes how the Partisans retreated carrying off by force many children who never saw their families again. If these are her feelings, why is the story so biased towards Communism?

The parents of 11-year-old Andi are engaged in guerrilla activity, heroically fighting their cause in the mountains. Her grandmother tells her, "To be a communist is to want all good things for all people". The reader sympathises with the family and the difficulties under which they live. The fact that communists teach atheism is ignored. They are deemed hand-in-glove with the nominal state religion, which is probably true but beyond the comprehension of young readers.

The author's overall thrust is the violence and futility of war, but compared with *Nothing Else Matters* in a similar setting, Rosen's treatment is very negative. The monarchist police-force are portrayed as the villains, but no justice is seen to be done on either side. Andi's mother and brother are killed and her grandmother receives "an ugly gash across her forehead" from the police-chief's knife.

If the message here is that children are the innocent victims of war, who cannot be blamed for copying the aggression of their elders, this principle should have been applied also to the police-chief's son, who is portrayed as a bully. Andi yells at him, "… you are not fit to lick a dog's ass". Rival gangs of pre-adolescents clash in the cemetery at midnight, indicating a breakdown of discipline and parental control. The anarchic spirit says, "I will do as I please".

In *Andi's War*, the enemy is anyone who stands for an ideal which is not your own. In *Nothing Else Matters* the enemy is anyone who is against *you*. That does not include Moomi, the Muslim orphan adopted by the family, nor the Druze woman in labour whom they help on Christmas Day. The fact that the Christian Party-leader bemoans the absence of parliament, the judiciary, authority, security and freedom, indicates these are desirable aspects of a stable peace-time government.

Much as we abhor war and suffering, we must accept that the spiritual battle will inevitably be reflected in the world and in literature. Pacifism is an attractive option, but propaganda in favour of world peace is more likely to be New Age wishful thinking than a genuine concern for one's neighbour.

3:1) Are children being seduced by campaigns with ulterior motives?

Peace and harmony are often promoted by ecological campaigns like Greenpeace and the World Wild Life Fund for Nature. However it takes only a little investigation to discover some worrying aspects of the green movement which attracts a following as diverse as feminism and Buddhism. Undoubtedly many of its supporters have a sincere concern for conservation of the planet. Still, it is important to realise that these are areas where great discernment is needed because deception is rife.

How could anyone be suspicious of such a widely acceptable, even "Christian", ideal as the care of the environment?! Well, let's consider the first Green Consumer Exhibition of 1990. Included in its entrance fee was a free ticket for the Mind-Body-Spirit Festival in the adjacent hall.

This five-day event featured all manner of psychic, occult and New Age activities. Its list of exhibitors included: Penguin and Unwin Hyman books, Aurora Crystals, Montessori Society AMI, the Findhorn Foundation (New Age), Mother Nature Centre and many others. Alternative medicine, inner exploration, and faith-healing mingled with healthy eating and world peace displays. The highlight of the convocation was a fifteen minute pause so that all could participate in a public healing of the planet.

Alongside works on organics, recycling and rainforests, adult titles of a more dubious kind in the "Green Books" category include those about Gaia, the Animate Earth, spiritual activism, feminism, nature worship, eastern religion and magic.

It is obvious that the green movement is attracting those searching for a spiritual dimension, but have been diverted into what is termed "creation-centred spirituality". The focus is on the created rather than the Creator. Followers speak of a "Cosmic Christ" and teach that creation will "be healed when a spiritual harmony is achieved". They seek healing of the environment rather than the salvation of sinners in preparation for the new heaven and the new earth.

Green writers are keen to convey their beliefs to the younger generation. Juliet Solomon, author of *Green Parenting*, observes that the images assimilated by the young are lost from the conscious mind by the age of 6-7, but later form "the unconscious basis of conscious judgements and actions". What better reason for allowing only good seed to be sown!

There are many "green" books being published for children as authors jump on this bandwagon. Many will appear to be harmless, but be alert to conditioning phrases like "saving the planet". One green list included *Barbar's Yoga* (by L. de Brunhoff) as a teaching tool for youngsters. Some, like *Dust on the Mountain* by Ruskin Bond, will be genuinely attempting to portray man's excesses – here, the exploitation of the forest. Rich men from the cities are blamed for buying up the land, selling the deodars for furniture and houses, and tapping the pines to death for their resin. In this story the tree is the champion, as a lone specimen breaks the fall of a runaway truck hurtling over a precipice.

Others, like *Spellhorn*, will use the "back to nature" theme as a vehicle for alternative philosophies – man at one with the animals, primitive origins to be regained. The Old Woman complains that man has spoiled the world. She says, "The Unicorn gives us eyebright". By this she means the power to understand environmental problems. Laura, who is blind, is not only healed physically by the presence of the Unicorn, but is also gifted with psychic insight. In *Swiftly Tilting Planet*, Gaudior with his healing crystal horn accuses, "Your planet does not deal gently with lovers of peace". The readers' sympathies are aroused.

C4.0) Are children being targeted by social campaigns in an unethical manner?

The sentiments at the heart of Animal Rights campaigns are akin to those of the environmental issue. Once again, Christians would share in a caring attitude towards God's creatures, yet would balk at the strategies that some fanatics use for publicity's sake, even going as far as contaminating food or planting bombs.

If children are to read propagandist material from such campaigners, they need opportunities to discuss this emotive subject in a balanced way with careful parental guidance. The methods used by fiction writers make quite an impact on those who, being young, feel a natural attraction towards animals. Passionate feelings are stored as deep-seated impressions, though the capacity of minors to make reasoned judgements is not yet fully developed.

Ruth Brown's *The Grizzly Revenge* is promoted in the Children's Book Magazine Online as being for infants/ juniors aged 5-8. At first glance it appears to be about a cruel Ruler and his crazy wife, yet it soon becomes clear that here is a strong statement in favour of animal rights. The couple, who have spent their lives hunting creatures large and small, are alarmed to find the crocodile bag and bearskin cape return to life, only to strangle and devour their owners. The crocodile is gruesomely depicted with blood dripping from his lips as he eats the final limb! Such vengeful ideas are dangerous since they could incite youngsters to take the wrong kind of action, that of using violence on behalf of poor defenceless creatures. For a happy ending, the castle becomes a paradise for animals, humans never more to venture near – "No pain and fear, just peace and life".

Before being carried away by this fanciful idea, one should consider God's decree in Genesis 1:26-28, in which mankind as the crown of creation is commissioned to rule over the animal kingdom and cultivate the earth. Any suggestion that animals are of *more* value than people is not in accordance with God's purpose for the stewardship of his world. Perhaps a change in the Ruler's heart would have been a better moral.

Vegetarianism is the logical outcome of the reverence for animals which originates from eastern religion. Rather than being concerned for their quality of life, Dahl implies in *The B.F.G.* that we should not eat pigs since they have done us no harm. Actually, God declared at the time of his covenant with Noah that people *may* eat meat, and Jesus later confirmed this (Gen.9:3, Mark 7:19).

Dahl is quite a campaigner, though in his tale of *Danny, Champion of the World* it is not clear whether his anti-pheasant-breeding stand is from pity for the birds or hatred of the rich landowners on whom he unleashes a passionate tirade. He appeals to the social conscience as he protests that the cost of rearing one bird is equal to the price of one hundred loaves. In fact, Danny and his dad are intent on capturing the birds for their own use!

Controversy arises when the issues are not clear-cut. Perhaps the best treatment is to present both sides fairly. There are some good examples. *Trouble, the Fox* from the *Ginn Reading Scheme* takes an anti-foxhunting stance, but an equal case is put in support of the angry farmers whose chickens are stolen.

Mrs Frisby and the Rats of Nimh is an enthralling story from Robert O'Brien which focuses the attention on animal experimentation. Rather than a vindictive approach, the author makes the point that the creatures are not maltreated, merely scared of captivity and the unknown. As a result of their laboratory programming, they develop into a breed of super-intelligent Rats who escape to live a semi-human existence with all modern conveniences.

They hold no bitterness against their captors, in fact they enjoy their raised standard of living until their conscience warns them they are being caught up in a materialistic "people-race". They are living a life "so easy that it (seems) pointless". They also realise their dependence on stolen goods has earned them a bad reputation. Their decision to renounce it all in favour of a simple, agricultural life-style, hastened on by the arrival of the exterminators, makes a point about pollution and is applauded by the reader who by now is cheering for the Rats!

4.1) Is the author jumping on the latest bandwagon to ensure credibility?

4.2) Does the book promote the use of alcohol or drugs of any kind?

When propaganda is, by general consensus, considered to be a "good cause", it is more likely to be termed "social education". There is no doubt that capturing the public's attention and targeting the area of concern produces a fair measure of success.

However, some authors seem to be bending over backwards to include the right ingredients solely to ensure acceptance by publishers and critics. It is as though, by jumping on the latest bandwagon, they feel certain of popular credibility. In a few cases, one suspects the hope that a plethora of social messages will conceal contraband smuggled in unnoticed.

Love or hate the works of Judy Blume, it must be admitted that she scores highly on the bandwagon count! In *Blubber*, the bully protests about the fur trade, collects for UNICEF, and states that "smoking is dangerous to your health", whilst her father points out the foolishness of carrying knives. In *Then Again, Maybe I Won't*, Blume speaks out against fast driving, underage drinking, smoking and stealing, but the young reader identifies with Tony and his sexual gratification.

Of greatest concern to parents in recent years have been the dangers of addictive substances. Much has been done in schools to tackle the problem. Books like *Grange Hill Rebels*, published back in 1987, have climbed on this bandwagon in condemning drug-taking and certainly its graphic descriptions –

"Brainless morons stewing in their own juice …cold and shivering …sores on their faces …in the gutter …unemployable …"

– must have had the desired effect.

It is amazing therefore that one can still find harmful messages regarding these issues between the covers of children's novels. Reference is made to a poet in *An Ash-Blond Witch* who enjoys a "sort of hallucinatory trip" which causes him to write beautiful poetry. *Dragon Paths* is more explicit. "Opium was for the pleasure of the masters, to smoke a calming pipeful on a cool evening". Yumi justifies drug-peddling because as a cripple it is the only way to make money. Many unemployed youngsters could use a similar excuse! He warns Tomi against involvement, but only because it is dangerous. That is tantamount to a dare! As Yumi passes him a package he says, "Here smell! It's good."

In *Tipper Wood's Revenge*, fifteen-year-old Rick seems to be a chain-smoker; his cigarettes are mentioned quite unnecessarily five times in the first six pages: "Rick came running up, cigarette still hanging from his lips". His friend Tipper wished he had that much money to spend! Although Rick is actually the informer, this fact is kept concealed until the final twist in the story. Tipper himself comes across in a fairly positive light. Was it necessary then to bolster his image with a half-pint of lager? In view of the problems of underage drinking, this would have been better omitted.

Similar irresponsibility is shown by *Cyril Bonhamy* who drinks not one but several large glasses of champagne at his reward ceremony. Frankie's mum (in *Frankie's Dad*), who goes out "on the razzle" when her difficulties weigh too heavily, demonstrates the abuse of alcohol as an escape route.

Those who care must be watchful! Is the good work that is being done by social education being undermined by subtle counter-influences from fictional characters? The "good guys", and those with whom the readers can identify, carry the most weight. Alternatively, if the message is clumsily overstated or inserted gratuitously, readers will become anaesthetised, recognising the propaganda for what it is, even rebelling against it.

C5.0) Is the promotion of equality in accordance with Christian teaching?

Surely equality is a Christian concept? All people, though sinful, were worth dying for and have equal value in God's sight (John 3:16). That is not to say that we are all the same, nor should we assume that all interpret equality in the same way. It was God's intention that in our individuality we would complement one another, each with different roles and abilities. People are now more aware of the evils of prejudice based on attributes which cannot be changed. Indeed, race, colour, and gender are God-given and all people are part of the tapestry of creation.

As for class distinction, this is an awareness inborn into much of the world's population. Whilst the Bible teaches social justice, Jesus recognised that the poor would always be with us (Mat.26:11) and did not attempt to bring down rulers. The Christian way is to promote mutual respect for one another, whether of high rank or lowly station, to work for the good of others, and to care for their well-being. God's desire is for us to be content and to find our self-esteem, not through wealth, social standing or even education, but through knowing his love personally.

In recent years, the reaction against discrimination in the name of civil rights has led to drastic changes in literature. Let's first consider whether, in spite of media coverage and diligent campaigning, there is still any prejudice in children's books.

5.1) Is there any sexist bias?

Those who have worked so hard for women's rights would wish to instil anti-sexist ideals into children from the beginning. Surely all would champion the cause of equal opportunities for girls as well as boys. Could any prejudice on the grounds of gender still exist?

As a boy, Roald Dahl (as recorded in his auto-biographical *Boy*) was terrified of his school matron. Was it that fear, or even hatred, which re-surfaced as he later created his female characters? One senses a sadistic pleasure in his description of the aunts in *James and the Giant Peach*, referring to them as "two ghastly hags". Aunt Sponge has a white flabby face "like a great white soggy over-boiled cabbage". From behind, Aunt Spiker gives the impression of being a pretty girl, but the reader receives a shock when her true ugliness is seen. Did Dahl harbour a suspicion that women are two-faced?

He develops the same theme in *The Witches*, where the Grand High Witch, in the presence of her cronies, removes her glamorous mask to reveal a demonic countenance. We sense the boy's panic as he witnesses the spectacle. "These females are actually talking about how to kill me", he quails. Are women and witches the same in Dahl's eyes? He explains that witches are always women and that the English ones are the most vicious of all. In his attempt to expose them, the whole congress is depicted without shoes, gloves and wigs; their corporate baldness is the supreme humiliation.

Is his exaggeration of the coarseness of women a means of fighting back? Even though he chooses *Matilda* as a heroine, it seems that Dahl is not at ease with her. She holds an awesome power in her eyes. At the climax of the tale she is abandoned by her parents and left in the care of her teacher. Significantly, the closest relationship that Dahl describes is between a boy and his *father*, in *Danny, Champion of the World*.

When considering sexism it must be said that militant feminism has a tendency to regard the opposite sex with disdain! The hen-pecked image is degrading to all concerned and is certainly not a positive substitute for the repression of women. The changing roles of men and women have already been discussed in chapter 6, but now let's look at the motivation behind the promotion of anti-sexism.

5.2) Is the anti-sexist lobby using propaganda for dubious aims?

At the beginning of *Harry's Horse*, by Sheila Lavelle, there is a picture of mum reading the newspaper at the breakfast table whilst dad cooks the eggs and bacon. Neither of these activities is surprising in itself, but in juxtaposition, a point is obviously being made with great effect. The author is making the statement, "I am not a sexist writer".

At the same time she is exchanging one negative for another by suggesting the reversal of roles with an underlying element of revenge on the mother's part. The author intends to evoke a response that questions why mothers should slave in the kitchen. Surely a more positive image would show the whole family sharing the tasks. Shirley Hughes' *Bathwater's Hot* is a good example. The breaking away from stereotypes is to be applauded but in attempting to redress the balance the pendulum can swing too far.

The assertion of a girl's right to excel in male-dominated occupations begins even at the picture-book level with such titles as *Miss Brick the Builders' Baby* and *Mrs Plug the Plumber* (Mr Plug is the plumber's mate), both by Allan Ahlberg. Most would agree that girls should have the opportunity to enjoy excitement as much as boys. However, as this movement develops it begins to lose sight of the values of distinct femininity and masculinity. In *Andi's War*, a girl is the tough gang-leader. In *Golden Journey*, Eleni displays an almost masculine ability to "rough it". Even when dressed in the Princess's gown it is obvious that she is "lean and muscular" and only too happy to don her tunic again.

In promoting the liberation of girls, are writers allowing the repression of boys? The trend in modern stories is for an older and therefore stronger girl to protect or rescue a younger boy: in *Ghost-Eye Tree*, the sister is braver than her small brother.

Indeed, are children being denied the opportunity to develop fully the special attributes of their own gender? If little Mary is allowed the excitement of a toy train, but deprived of the pleasure of a doll, then no advance has been made. If she is not taught how to care for the doll, and Johnny is not given responsible role-models, then society as a whole is the loser.

5.3) Is any racial prejudice evident?

"Do not ill-treat a foreigner or oppress him".   (Exodus 22:21)

The success of the campaign for racial equality cannot be ignored. Whether or not it has really changed people's attitudes is arguable, but it has achieved legislation against discrimination and an acknowledgement that we live in a multi-cultural society. It is interesting to note the effect this has had on writers who as a whole seem to have a pre-occupation with this theme.

Writers are so keen for a multi-cultural image that their inclusion of the correct ethnic mix seems contrived. Rather than a random scattering of races, we find a well-thought-out balance intended to offend no-one. In the story of *The Bracelet*, the heroine is Indian, the teacher Afro-Caribbean, whilst the bad girl is blond. *The Friends of Pine Street* gang include Daniel who is black and Sharon who is a clever *and* beautiful Pakistani. The West Indian family who play only a small part in *The Key to the Other* wallow in positive images, right down to their expensive trainers!

Is it really necessary for Frankie to be born of a Jamaican father (*Frankie's Dad*)? It would have made no difference to the story if he were Scottish, except there would not have been the opportunity to compare the pale and pimply step-father with Dad who is black and beautiful *and* unconcerned about racists. Frankie gives as good as she gets when she suffers insults and aggression from her peers. Rough as she is, Frankie is the one who protects the snivelling, bed-wetting Jass from the violent abuse of his father.

In the attempt to be fair to people of other cultures and to explain their beliefs and customs, there is the danger of some discrimination against the indigenous population and the Christian faith. It seems the best heroes must have an ethnic friend! The situation is less artificial when the main purpose of the book is to make a positive statement about race relations. *Fiona Finds Her Tongue* by Diana Hendry, illustrates how a shy girl's problem can be solved by her helping a Vietnamese boy to speak English.

Come a Stranger not only gives a sympathetic portrayal of a black girl, Mina, growing up and experiencing prejudice, but pursues the plight of minorities in general. Dicey is a white girl who is a loner. "She stood apart from the others by choice and so others were keen to humiliate her". When Louis wants to invite one white friend to his party, his mother is concerned that she will feel awkward. A positive message is given about all colours being the same underneath, but not all having the same experience of life.

The point made regarding Dicey and Mina both coming from Christian homes is a good one, similarly that in *Grandma's Favourite* by Peter Heaslip in which the family of a mixed marriage holds a Christening party. All too often in books it is assumed that people of other races cannot be Christian, but that of course is false. Neither should it be assumed that Jesus was white!

In spite of the over-emphasis on racial harmony, offensive passages are still found in children's books. In *The Golden Journey*, the Governor casts aspersions on half-castes and recommends they be destroyed at birth. In *Elidor*, Paddy is the stereotyped Irishman, rough and drunk. A passer-by comments, "Ruddy Micks!" Is it helpful to perpetuate these images?

From a Christian perspective, anti-racist messages should aim to counteract fear brought on by ignorance, and also to encourage justice and a respect for humanity. Stories about ethnic families in ordinary situations are perhaps the most helpful. Penny Dale's *Bet You Can't* shows that West Indian children are just as untidy as any others and react in the same way to clearing up. *But Martin!* by J.Counsel, develops in an amusing way the fact that we are all different, even in ability and the way we travel to school, but none are so strange as the Green Alien!

5.4) Is there any stereotyping of lifestyles according to social class?

Since the 1960s there has been an attempt to break away from the stereotyped middle-class family who kept their offspring in the nursery while young, and later in a boarding school, with riding lessons in the hols! Recently Enid Blyton has been enjoying a reprieve after suffering years of rejection by public libraries. During her absence the shelves became filled with many works of a lower standard, in the name of open-mindedness and equality.

Exchanging what may have seemed like the superficiality of the rich for the down-to-earth circumstances of the poor has simply resulted in further stereotyping! Philippa Pearce used old-fashioned names for the stars of *The Elm Street Lot* –Vera, Bert, Maisie, Jimmy – perhaps to emphasise the unfashionable nature of their dilapidated terraced community.

Leila Berg was one of the early pioneers in the field of working-class stories with her *Nippers Reading Scheme*. At Level 1, *Fish and Chips For Supper* condescendingly suggested that Dad was so lazy, or work-shy, that his family must live with naked light-bulbs and washing lines over the stairs. The implication here is that his poverty was his own fault. There is no reason why "lower class" should be equated with lower moral standards, or that low income should be associated with bad grammar, yet these are often used to typify the life-style.

Mary Hoffman brings out the point, in *The Second-Hand Ghost,* that children are aware of differing standards of living. Sarah's smart clothes are more of a barrier to her friendship with Lisa than race or colour would have been. In fact, Lisa's two friends are West Indian. She has a chip on her shoulder about being hard-up. It is typical of the current supernatural climate that it is the ghost in the pocket of her jumble-sale jacket which solves the problem!

Nadya Smith includes another much-maligned group, the gypsies, in her book *Imran's Secret*. The author intends to show Muslim children in a favourable light and explain some of their Asian ways. Unfortunately, in attempting to portray two distinct minorities as comrades in adversity overcoming their squabbles, some rather forthright opinions are given regarding the travelling people. Jaswinder considers them dirty, ragged and noisy. Her mother calls them thieves and liars. She is proved right when a gypsy boy steals a ball!

Since people are anything but equal financially, with some overworked whilst others are unemployed, it is important that literature promotes an understanding and tolerance of many valid life-styles, applying the principles of caring and sharing. As we have seen in this chapter, propaganda can be powerful. Let *us* also, parents, teachers and others who care, be encouraged to campaign for raised standards in young fiction. This does not mean a return to upper-class unreality, but challenges the downward trend from excellence as self-perpetuating rather than inspirational.

Recommended Books

For Younger Readers

Snowy Day by E.J. Keats.

Ladybird, Ladybird by Ruth Brown.

Michael and the Jumble-Sale Cat by M. Newman.

For Older Readers

The Friendship and Other Stories by M. D. Taylor.

Plots and Players by P. Melnikoff.

When Hitler Stole Pink Rabbit by Judith Kerr.

Why the Whales Came by Michael Morpurgo.

Latchkey Children by E. Allen.

Chapter 8: HORROR, DANGER AND DISTRESS

"Have nothing to do with the fruitless deeds of darkness, but rather expose them."   (Eph. 5:11–12).

D) Does the book portray violence or horror in a manner which is harmful to children?

Your scimitar shatters on the beast's head. "With a grunt, the creature charges --- impaling you on several of its bony horns and then crushing you against the walls of the pit. Your adventure is over."

(*Seas of Blood* by Jackson and Livingstone)

Many parents will protest confidently (or hopefully) that, appalling as this material may be, "My child doesn't read such rubbish!"

Then what about this one? –

Grendal ate his victim – "tore him limb from limb and swallowed him whole, sucking the blood in streams, crunching the bones…."

One more gory story from the latest horror comic? No, merely another exciting tale from a school reading scheme (and available on the internet) – level 13 of the Ginn 360 programme entitled *The Legends of Man* by Ian Serraillier. In book 4 of the same series, an excerpt from *The Day it Rained Forever* (by Ray Bradbury) offers this strange yet horrific description of a knight being run over by a steam train! –

"The dragon hit, spilled him over, down, ground him under. Passing, the black brunt of its shoulder smashed the remaining horse and rider thirty yards against the side of a boulder, wailing, wailing, the dragon shrieking".

Ironically, that passage expresses the problem perfectly. Violence is invading the child's world, threatening his very life. Though parents may try to monitor their children's internet viewing and block unsuitable television programmes, through literature there is still an open channel for violent images to reach our youngsters behind our backs, from between the covers of the most innocent of titles.

Who would guess that *The Swan* by Roald Dahl (from his collection of short stories *The Wonderful Story of Henry Sugar*), might contain a similar horror. A small boy is the object of torture for two brutish hooligans who obviously take great satisfaction in their callous deeds. There is no respite from the torment. Peter is tied between railway lines to await an oncoming train:

"It was as though a gun had gone off in his head. And with the explosion came a tearing, screaming wind that was like a hurricane blowing down his nostrils and into his lungs. The noise was shattering. The wind choked him. He felt as though he were being eaten alive…"

Amazingly he survives, only to be subjected to a further ordeal involving the death of a swan. What sort of mind could imagine such a gruesome story? Young people are being conditioned to regard aggression as normal and horror as exciting entertainment.

D1.0) Is there a generally aggressive atmosphere in the author's work?

1.1) Is the aggression or violence portrayed as normal, rather than an intrusion to be resisted?

Even in the domestic comedy we find thinly-veiled aggression permeating family life which goes beyond friendly banter. There may not be outright rudeness, but a generally abrasive atmosphere. In *The Shrieking Face* by Hazel Townson, the mother's irritable nature invites a similar response from her children. She turns on the toddler. "Shut up, you big spoilt baby!" she cries viciously. "You're always on the moan".

The normality of aggression is underlined by Frankie's Mum (in *Frankie's Dad*) when she says of Billy's violence towards Jass, "That's his right, he's his father!" Her own temper is not restrained when the boy breaks some plates. She shakes him by the shoulders till "his head wobble(d) on the end of his neck like the head of a rag doll" and exclaims, "Moronic little twerp … cretin". This could be deemed child abuse.

In *Joe Eats Bugs*, Susannah Gretz shows how mentally cruel children can be to one another. The two bullies, one white, the other black, accuse Joe of eating bugs in his sandwiches. We sense his panic, until he turns the tables on them, thus restoring his status in the pecking order. Even in the name of a friendship pact Flip, in *The Key to the Other,* promises to throw Nick off the pier one day, as though it would be wimpish to be too nice!

The message delivered is that aggression is the only way, whether for good or ill. Why does Hogarth's father take his double-barrelled shot-gun to protect himself against the *Iron Man*, whose only appetite is for metal objects? When Dahl's Danny is brutally caned in such graphic detail that the reader protests at the harshness of the punishment, his father threatens to kill the teacher! "Good" characters, whose initial reactions are aggressive rather than controlled, persuade young readers of the legitimacy of this kind of response.

In weighing the violent nature of any book, it is not simply a matter of counting the number of horrific incidents. Perhaps an attitude of conflict hangs over the whole scenario. This is true of *Island of the Strangers*. The atmosphere is dominated by the murderous spirit of the local legendary bandit. Maybe the authoress felt that a story set in Ireland must reflect the troubles there, but the boundaries of its influence are unlimited. The constant aggression has nothing to do with religion! It begins with Orla throwing an apple core at a party of visiting school-children and a feud ensues. Mrs. Egg, who never takes to strangers, calls them "a pack of city savages" and resents them picking the blackberries! Two boys, armed with a spade-shaft, go seeking a fight with the visitors. They attack one, who happens to be a girl, rubbing her face in the "sludgy black sand of the harbour bottom". "Eat dirt!" they taunt. Orla protests, though unconvincingly.

Nora, the heroine, refuses to take part in Brendan's Defence Force. We share her pain as she is accused of being a traitor. The young reader will also feel sorry for Brendan, though he is a bully, when all the grown-ups are against him, just because he made a gun – but it was only for show! No comment is made about him vandalising the visitors' minibus. In this setting, the reader expects violence as a normal way of life; it is not regarded as the intrusion into peace that must be resisted.

Further conditioning occurs with a book like *Myths and Legends* by R.Hunt, one of the *Oxford Junior Readers*, in which a high proportion of the tales, ten out of fifteen in this case, have a violent or tragic theme. In this one book we have a Javan story in which a woman kills her grandson and tries to persuade her son to kill his wife, who eventually drowns herself; a queen who poisons her husband's mistress out of jealousy; the disaster of Atlantis; the violent death of Balder; and the implication, in *But Lisa*, that Jake is glad to be rid of his wife in the river.

I accept that these are *old* legends, but it is disturbing that they have now been collected together for a school reading scheme. To include a preponderance of such material leads a child to concentrate on unwholesome ideas and excludes the balance which is more typical of life. Its effect is not far removed from books like *The Moon of Gomrath* which move continually from one horror to the next. The heroes are always under threat, with no respite, no space for "whatsoever things are admirable or praiseworthy…" (Phil.4:8-9). Such an onslaught of violent images must have a desensitising influence which, rather like a drug, creates a hunger which is more difficult to satisfy.

1.2) Is there a gradual build-up of violence or horror, inducing an expectation which needs to be satisfied?

Master of Fiends employs this technique to build up the tension and encourage an expectancy for increasingly horrific scenes. Horror, often associated with violence but not necessarily, is a violation against the mind and feelings, in other words, the soul. Hill's book opens with a relatively tame description of two demons: "…skin was scaly with long sparse hair smeared with filth and foulness that gave off a poisonous stink". The narrative continues in this vein, until the climax of the chapter when the fiends attack Jarral, "their red eyes flaring and fanged jaws gaping wide".

This becomes a predictable pattern a violent or frightening final paragraph to every chapter, urging the reader on, from one terrifying monster to the next. There is no real plot. All is associated with violent death. Chapter 6 observes, "Nothing had tried to kill them for some time". Be assured, there is not long to wait! Identifying with Jarral, the reader fears what the ultimate torture might be. "Soul-rending grief howl(s) through his being" as he discovers the worst − to be prevented from dying, but imprisoned at the point of death forever: eternal anguish with no release!

Less obvious, but equally effective in stimulating an appetite for horror, is the gradual increase of frightening incidents throughout a whole series or reading scheme. One does not need to turn to the blatantly spine-chilling thrillers for examples. Spooky houses and ghostly games at the lower levels of Sheila McCullagh's *One, Two, Three and Away Scheme* prepare a basic vocabulary for more disturbing adventures developed later in the *Humming Bird* extension readers.

Let's look in more detail at this strategy in another of her series – *Tim and Tobias.* Teachers have welcomed this scheme for its ability to capture the interest of reluctant readers. In the first book (A1), Tim is alone in the house when the lights go out. Unrealistically, he climbs into the attic to find something to read! He picks up a magic key which empowers Tobias the Cat to materialise. Tim is told, "There are Hidden People everywhere, only you can't see them – unless you have the key". The author creates an exciting atmosphere which compels the reader to move on to the next level. Unfortunately, the carrots used are horror and the supernatural, which can also be scary. Let us follow through the elements of the first theme and return to the second in a later chapter.

At the first level, Tobias becomes a familiar figure and a few of the Hidden People are introduced. In A4, Tim immediately assumes the stranger on the bridge is one of these invisible friends. What would a child with an active imagination learn from this? After a half-hearted comment that "you should be careful with strangers", he suggests that Tim meets him at midnight, with the promise of being home by morning!

Level 2 introduces the terrible Stump People, pictured in B2 with their green eyes peering out of their tree-trunk bodies. They appear on the cover of B3 together with a tiger pouncing. Tim is out in the dark again when a ghost attempts to poison him. Eventually (B8), Tim is attacked not only by a Stump Man but also by a wolf.

At level 3 most of the action is taking place at night, with the *frightening* aspect of ghosts and witches being emphasised. By the final set there has been sufficient reference to the terrifying Wind Witches to scare readers into imagining their presence in every storm or high wind. As the climax draws near, Tim encounters first the deadly spider, which he must avoid or smash with a club (D4, D6), and then the Stone Monsters. In D7, he is persuaded to go on alone and in the dark to rescue his friends from their stone prisons. Such a format, increasing the fear step by step, exploits the child's fascination with horror. Boys particularly, with their more aggressive personalities, will savour these images and allow them to dwell in the mind.

St.Paul describes the battle over sin as a battle for the mind, because the mind rules the body (Eph.4:22-24). A surfeit of horror attacks the mind directly, persuading it to indulge in thoughts of evil. Violent language often provokes violent actions. The apostle urges: "let the *Word of Christ* dwell in you richly" (Col.3:16), in order to be motivated by righteousness and truth. This produces self-control and real peace.

1.3) Does the book contain gratuitous violence or horror?

In former years a child's novel could have been relied upon to follow a story-line, maybe the resolving of a problem, a quest, or a voyage of discovery in the widest sense. The encountering of evil would have been seen as an interruption, a hindrance to the plot. Only such violence as was necessary to overcome the enemy was employed, usually just before the climax, allowing time for the reader to release the tension and enjoy the happy ending.

Nowadays we frequently find gratuitous violence and horror far beyond the requirements of the plot. Why does the hero of *The Dumb Cake* have such blood-thirsty thoughts? Isn't this a light-hearted tale of women scheming to catch a husband by superstitious ritual? Yet Parrot is overcome by a passionate desire to cut Betty into pieces, "to be the destroying angel, killing and killing until … he'd survey the bloody wreckage and empty out the last of the vials of wrath"!

Helen Cresswell's *Moondial* is creepy enough with its ghosts and their secret powers. Was it really necessary to overplay the horror of mental and spiritual cruelty inflicted on Sarah, just because of her purple birthmark? Surely there was a subtler way of making the point than to curse her. "If ever you look into a mirror … the devil would get you", hissed the terrible voice of old Mrs Crump. Tom's response is equally savage: "…hope she does throw a fit and foams at the mouth and her eyes drop out!" Consider the effect these passages would have on readers afflicted either with birthmarks or epilepsy. Consider the ammunition given to children who seek power in tormenting others!

Some works suffer from enhancement of the text by over-enthusiastic illustrators. Again, we are not only concerned with the ghastly motifs of the *Fighting Fantasy* game-books, where three or four designs are used repeatedly, stamping images of skulls and monsters on the mind. Younger children will be alarmed to unexpectedly come across a nasty picture of a hangman and his noose, with vicious dogs snarling at the hero of *Hey Robin*. This book by Robert Leeson is written in the style of the traditional folk-tale.

Similarly, *Teeny Tiny and the Witch-Woman* by Barbara Walker *could* have been the moral tale of three foolish brothers who lose their way in the woods and, ignoring their mother's warning, are taken in by a wicked witch. They escape when Teeny Tiny plays a clever trick and his brothers learn a lesson.

However, illustrator Michael Foreman has transformed this picture-book into something else. The witch is described as "a strange old woman …with her nose turned down and her chin turned up and just the points of her teeth showing … she beckoned with her bony finger", but the picture shows a horror character with green warty skin and talons, giving a reptilian appearance. She sharpens a huge knife, drawn life-size, eight inches long across the page. Another "short, sharp knife" is depicted with a skull on the handle, spooky figures hide in the beams, and the trees have ghastly faces. This exaggeration of disturbing images is quite unwarranted.

In the two examples that follow, the authors have used their opening paragraphs to entice readers with a promise of more to come. *It's Too Frightening For Me* (Shirley Hughes) is a slim volume, obviously for younger or backward readers. From the cover and first few pages, we anticipate at least a ghost story. The publicity blurb sets the scene: "A deserted house, a face at the window, and some blood-curdling screams". Children will, as intended, expect to find a witch in residence. In fact, she is merely an old lady in a house too big for her. This is a simple humorous story in an unnecessarily deceptive wrapper.

On the other hand, *Tipper Wood's Revenge* holds no empty promises. Its first three paragraphs have been deliberately positioned to capture the attention of the prospective reader. Tommo has been discovered face-down in a pool of blood. Then comes the flash-back to the previous events of the day, but soon, by the sixth page, Tipper himself is being attacked. The hero is not above violent thoughts of his own. When he sees the thug, he wants to smash his face into the ground. When questioned by the police Tipper has a sudden desire to "get out and break a window". This is a typical detective thriller with a good plot, but it is also the story of street-wise kids used to conflict.

It has to be faced that many people enjoy horror themes, whether on film or in books. Authors of this persuasion are teaching the young how to derive the same pleasure. They are writing for the sole purpose of indulging in horror. Jane Holiday encourages the 8+ age-group to enjoy this form of entertainment. Her family of vampires, in *Gruesome and Bloodsocks Move House*, are portrayed as ordinary people setting up home in a tower-block. You can almost catch the "loathsome smell of fresh blood" as they sally forth on their nightly expeditions.

The compulsion felt by many to pursue this excitement is mirrored by the activity of the children in *The Key to the Other*. They feel strangely compelled to follow the Evil Door, as though under a spell, meeting no hindrance from their parents! Nick is almost strangled by a vacuum-cleaner monster. Flip is attacked by metal hands. The frenzied chase becomes a nightmare of violence for the sake of it; for what other reason does a mysterious arm haul the poor ice-cream seller into his fridge?

At the fun-fair, the girls *want* to be frightened on the Ghost Train, thus challenging feebler readers! The horror of the scorpions crawling over their faces, in their hair and down their shirts can only be relieved by Nick's powers of hypnosis! Nick himself is viciously kicked, thrown, dragged and threatened with a cracked skull. These events are so improbable that they take one into the world of fantasy where, removed from reality, the reader is deceived into believing this is all great fun and safe to enjoy. The blurb states that this is a book for older children, but the colourful cover, extra-large print and slap-stick "comedy" will attract younger readers from eight upwards.

Some writers are seizing the opportunity to attract readership by taking advantage of a child's natural fascination with horror. The thrill of such books heightens the child's anticipation; if a text fails to live up to expectation, the reader feels dissatisfied. The notoriety of adventure game-books has led readers to expect the contents to be horrifying, perhaps shocking. Their writers are under an obligation to deliver the goods! The lurid covers announce the contents with pride, even rebellion against decency.

Aiken's *A Foot in the Grave* is a large eye-catching presentation which at first glance resembles a picture-book for the young. It is a far-fetched tale of digging up graves and disturbing the ghosts. The stories have been written as an interpretation of Jan Pienkowski's weird art-work, but on the whole are fairly anti-climactic. The most harmful line is slipped in as an aside: "I was watching the late, late horror film". The young reader will be tempted to satisfy his desire with more horrific material elsewhere.

1.4) Are there explicit descriptions of violence or horror beyond that of the child's own imagination or ability to cope, such as will affect behaviour?

Tempting youngsters further into horror *and* fantasy are the adventure game-books. Unaware of the contents, parents are often delighted that their sons are enjoying a renewed interest in the written word. Little do they realise that the most violent reactions are evoked from aspirant heroes who are lured onwards by the promise of excitement. The reader controls the plot and becomes deeply involved in the action. Here is an example from *Seas of Blood*.

As you encounter a Cyclops, you are given a choice. Will you a) jump up and down on its back, b) kick it in the ribs, or c) shoulder it in the head? Having chosen the latter, you are invited to take a flying kick at its mid-riff, its legs or its head. Taking the latter again, your choice leads to an upper-cut in the groin, "achieving little and badly bruising your hand". You then may choose to elbow it in the ribs, kick it in the armpit, punch it in the kidneys, or in the jaw, elbow smash to its arm, etc., etc., till you or the monster lose all your stamina points! ---

The overall plot is rather boring, just one punch up after another, but it surely must excite aggressive emotions in young boys. The common format of such books is first to set the scene and to establish the stamina, luck, wealth etc. of the player/reader according to a throw of the dice. The narrative consists of many short chunks of action, each culminating in either a decision for the reader to take, or a roll of the dice to determine the outcome. Several stories may be contained in one book, depending on the reader's choice of adventure. He may pursue a particularly violent option out of curiosity to know what happens next. There is a chart to record your score, accumulation of weapons and gold. From the immaturity of the handwriting left as evidence in library copies, the age of these combatants is from eight upwards.

The introduction to Ian Livingstone's *City of Thieves* expresses the wish that "the luck of the gods go with you". The aim is to fetch help from the wizard in the evil city against the terror of Zanbar Bone. The cast-list in itself is a catalogue of horror: a serpent-queen, a mummy, an ogre, a vampire, a spirit-stalker, hags, giant rats, Zombies, death-hawks and so on. In this role-playing fantasy, violence is felt personally.

"He produces a dagger from his ragged clothing and leaps at you. His wild eyes belong to a man insane or possessed and you must fight him".

There is no room here for pacifism, nor for the would be valiant knight: "She embraces you and slowly sinks her fangs into your neck to drink your blood. You drift into an unconscious sleep …when you awake …you have become a vampire yourself".

Children are invited to participate sadistically, even masochistically, savouring the details of various methods of inflicting pain. Whether their actions prove to be right, morally or otherwise, is rarely the issue. They are conditioned to react violently, even when it is unwarranted:

"A man wearing a white apron is sitting at a bench busily polishing a silver goblet".

One of the three options is to attack him with your sword!

These "games" of total involvement encourage a callous attitude towards those left in agony, whilst moving on to the next hair-raising encounter. Children are overwhelmed by an onslaught of cruelty which is obscene. Even in non-role-playing books explicit descriptions of horror come thick and fast:

"I ran hot lead in the marrow of their bones; they will die of it". (Serret, in *Wizard of Earthsea*)

"… a searing, sizzling sound as the giant was blinded … gave a terrible howl of a wounded beast… pulling the stake from his eye..." (Hero deals vengeance to Cyclops, in *Voyage of Odysseus*)

Children's literature has always contained violence, the giant having his head cut off, the invaders being flung over the battlements, but the impact of that horror could be held at arm's length. It was always controlled by the extent of the child's own experience or imagination. The will could be used as a safety valve.

Now, in striving to satisfy a lust for excitement and a fascination with the macabre, modern authors are tempted to be unnecessarily explicit, taking the child into a deeper realm of horror, beyond his own imagining. These graphic images are indelibly imposed upon the mind.

These may actually be pictorial images in books for younger or weaker readers. *Merlin the Wizard* is innocently positioned between *The Pied Piper* and *Dick Whittington* in the *Great Tales From Long Ago* series. However, Susan Hunter's colourful battle scenes on the first two pages are absolutely horrific: a large skull hangs over the sky; there is much blood in evidence on knives and bodies; one victim is about to be stabbed to death.

There is plenty of blood in *Andi's War*. Following a description of men staggering home from street-fighting, bleeding from knife wounds, there is a messy account of grandmother slaughtering a pig: "Every time she plunged the point of the knife into its neck it would leap into the air, crazy with fear, the blood gushing from the various wounds in thin jets colouring them both crimson". Is the purpose to portray the horror of violent death? When grandmother is attacked by the police-chief, every drop of blood is dwelt on, held close for a better view. By contrast, in *Nothing Else Matters*, horror is suggested but controlled – Farid "went on screaming, and covering his face … he could not see". Here the violence of war is not glorified, but portrayed with sadness.

When the violence is close to the reader's experience it makes more impact than when it is removed into the realms of fantasy, that is, unless the reader has been brought into the action through role-play. It may be argued that *adults* are able to cope with fictional horror, separating it from reality and using it as an outlet for pent-up aggressions. That may be so for the majority, but there are cases where individuals' lives have been destroyed because of an inability to step back again into the real world.

Michael Ryan, the Hungerford murderer, was engaged in a fantasy game by post at the time of the massacre. He had taken on the role of Phodius Tel, high priest to the evil serpent-god, Set. A month before that terrible day, he received this challenge: "You have been one of my greatest Terran priests and as such are worthy of the power I offer. But Phodius, you have one last point to prove. Can you kill your fellow Terrans? Will you accept, Phodius, to go back to Terra and slay them, to devour their soul in the name of Set the immortal god?" Two weeks later, the scene was set for him to act: "When at last you awake you are standing in a forest. There is a throbbing in your head, a madness that is the exhilaration of the serpent-god. You know what you must do. Know what power is to be gained from this". (Daily Mail 30/8/87).

If there are some adults who cannot distinguish between fact and fiction, how much more will children be confused, who often lapse into the world of imagination. From classroom displays, it is evident that gruesome, even violent, ideas are being reflected in art-work and creative writing. This is the outworking of something deeper.

Play is the natural way that children come to terms with adult behaviour and is also a means of pursuing the question, "What happens if…?" Children are quick to copy and experiment as part of the learning process, though lacking in wisdom and reason. Having received images of aggression from books and films, they will act out their heroes' adventures, those with a more vivid imagination directing the moves and even the speech of others.

Roy Bentley's aim, in *Space Crash*, to "forget the wars and monsters of science-fiction and present the cold reality of space – dangerous, difficult, but enormously challenging", is most laudable. However, the several large coloured pictures of the space-craft being crashed by a runaway supply-ship are actually very violent. One can imagine small boys re-enacting this drama amidst the scattered remains of broken toys!

Unfortunately, children have not yet learned to use the mental mechanisms which restrain their actions, neither do they know their own strength. Much fictional violence takes youngsters beyond their developmental ability to foresee the outcome.

When children live in a fantasy world filled with exemplary models, they will learn maturity through play. If however that world is one of aggression, then harmful attitudes will be reinforced and they will be a danger to themselves and others. Exclusions of pupils from school for bad behaviour are becoming much more common at primary levels. As they develop into adolescents and leave play behind, they will become part of the alarming statistics that prove increasing violence in the classroom and on the street, revealing itself in bullying, assault and even murder.

Remember the pagan principle that "dark defeats dark" (see chapter 3, section A6:2). People do horrible things just because they *are* horrible, to show bravado to their rivals. Arising out of this philosophy is the urge to prove oneself, to meet a challenge. How much can I bear before I waver?

This kind of strength is falsely equated with bravery; it is actually a form of power-seeking. For some youngsters, the desire to be as nasty as possible stems from a rebellion against convention or authority and is seen in their outrageous clothing or destructive behaviour. Sometimes these violent actions are even filmed and put out on the internet.

Young people brought up on role-playing books have become accustomed to *choosing* a course of action. If they have not been taught a clear moral code, there is no guarantee that their choice will be for good. They may well choose the evil way! The fact that an activity may be *enjoyed*, does not justify its practice. There *are* other criteria!

1.5) Is the book likely to frighten children?

Whether or not children ought to be frightened is a complicated issue. Fear is useful as a warning system, restraining us from impulsive or dangerous actions. On the other hand, we find the command, "Do not be afraid", many times in the Bible because fear can stunt growth and initiative.

Undoubtedly fear is an emotion with which children must gradually be helped to come to terms. Games played with toddlers, such as "this little pig", where the child anticipates being pounced on and tickled, are the first means of conveying the reassurance of loving parents ready with cuddles after a frightening experience. The same message is learned from Alice Dalgliesh's *The Bears on Hemlock Mountain*. The constant rhythmic refrain –

"There *are* no bears on Hemlock Mountain,

No bears at all.

Of course, there are no bears on Hemlock Mountain,

No bears, no bears, no bears, no bears at all.

– almost gives a fun quality to this story which I have had no qualms about using with 7-year-olds. Jonathan is suitably admonished for the tardiness which increased his danger, but is praised for his resourcefulness in using the cooking-pot to hide safely. His father comes to the rescue and mother provides the comfort.

Children at this stage of growing up do have fears, irrational or otherwise, and need to learn how to cope with them. A very helpful book which teaches through another's experience is *Alice Alone* by Shirley Isherwood. The heroine is left alone with her small brother when grandpa is called away for an unexpectedly long time to tend a lambing ewe in the snow. Alice shows a responsible attitude and overcomes her fear by planning what she can do and trusting for a happy ending to their predicament.

Those books which cause concern are the ones that thrust children into a world of frightening experiences which are beyond their ability to cope. Even though some want to be scared, it is actually more than they can handle. They think they will enjoy the excitement, but the explicit horror absorbed litters the mind with quantities of rubbish which are likely to lead to anxiety, nightmares and disturbed behaviour.

Rose Impey's "*Creepies*" series comes into this category. They feature children aged about 5-7 trying to scare themselves at night. Full-page pictures emphasise the text: I lie there afraid to move. An icy feeling is spreading all the way up my back". *The Flat Man* curls up in the corner, even creeps into bed! In *Scare Yourself to Sleep*, there are dustbin demons, giant stick insects and a cat that sucks its victim's blood. Children of this age have no discernment regarding the effect of such nasty images on the mind. The impact is greater when the horror impinges on the child's world, rather than being removed into a fantasy setting.

They Wait is a collection of spine-chillers by, according to the blurb, "six favourite children's writers" who "show you how eerie and frightening ordinary places can be – a bus shelter, a sea-side flat, a playground …" One of these stories, *A Prince in Another Place* by Philippa Pearce, begins with a suicide and ends with the devilish supply-teacher and the bully headmaster disappearing in an explosion, supposedly to hell. Another, *The Front Room* by Michelle Magorian, is about a girl haunted by a child-murderer in her bedroom: "The large shadow loomed nearer and she felt his hands grip her violently round the throat". What effect would such stories have on *your* daughter?

In *Run Cassie, Run* by Zena Carus, the setting is so familiar that we share the heroine's ordeal. Over six pages of tension-building narrative, a menacing group of louts surround the girl. "Cassie felt their breath on her cheeks and felt the pain of the iron railings on her back". Their threatening actions are suddenly interrupted when one of the gang has a near-fatal fall --- "a discarded body amongst the dustbins". Cassie believes she has caused his death and for the remainder of the book we flee with her from the guilt of murder. Her terror is increased as she finds herself, first in the middle of a riot, and later out all night in a freezing blizzard. The author intends 9-12 year-olds to experience Cassie's fear with her.

Many children are sensitive and vulnerable. They will not go out of their way to read frightening books, but *will* be affected by the unexpectedly gruesome episodes that appear gratuitously, like Dahl's recollection of having his adenoids removed at the dentist's without anaesthetic (*Boy*): "I was horrified by the huge red lumps that has fallen out of my mouth into the white basin and my first thought was that the doctor had cut out the whole of the middle of my head".

We must also remember the extra-sensitive child who will need special protection. I was once informed about a boy who uncharacteristically began wetting the bed. The cause was traced to Music and Movement lessons at school in which he was required to "be a ghost". When this activity ceased, so did the problem.

There will be some who are terrified by *Where the Wild Things Are*, even though all the monsters seem almost to be smiling. Here is an element of fantasy, even nonsense, which lightens the atmosphere and distances their threat: "they roared their terrible roars and gnashed their terrible teeth and rolled their terrible eyes and showed their terrible claws". They are likened to the wild part of human nature and convey a valuable message, but parents and teachers must be aware of those children who will find even these images upsetting.

Child psychologists are counselling increasing numbers of disturbed youngsters. Young Minds, the UK's leading charity committed to the mental health of youngsters, has reported that more than 850,000 children and young people have been diagnosed with mental health conditions and over 500,000 have a behavioural and emotional conduct disorder.

Professor Michael Rutter once told the Independent newspaper that more than 60% of children with conduct disorders have serious problems in adult life, including breakdowns and committing criminal offences.

Whereas liberal thinkers would say that enjoyment of horror and violence does no harm, Christians would maintain that it does no good to feed the darker side of human nature. We would do well to heed St. Paul's warning to "avoid every kind of evil" (1 Thess.5:22).

D2.0) Does the book portray dangerous situations irresponsibly?

Who would expect writers of young fiction to put their readers at risk of physical harm, yet this is actually happening through the bad example set by heroes and heroines. Many authors today write about children deliberately entering potentially dangerous situations, with no warning about the possible consequences. Such an irresponsible attitude is far too common. Many stories depict youngsters going out alone, particularly at night. *Paul, Sally and Little Grey*, and the Sheila McCullagh books have already been mentioned. Others include *Spellhorn, T.R.Bear*, and Owen Owen of *Tatty Apple* who spends the night out in the woods searching for his magic rabbit, but there are many more.

If children, *through no fault of their own*, have to fend for themselves, as in *Alice Alone,* and through courage and tenacity they are seen to triumph in adversity, then this is acceptable. Their being alone is reckoned as the exception rather than the rule. The reader hopes for a happy conclusion and the return to normality.

However, it is alarming to find *Little Pete* walking along a busy street on his own, helping a man to clean his car and then going for a ride with him. He only asks his mum's permission because the man told him to. What if he hadn't? Almost every one of the twelve chapters involves this small boy out alone, speaking to strangers and even entering their houses. Whilst out alone and beyond parental control, our fictional friends engage in all kinds of foolish escapades, full of potential danger. Paul and Sally find a horse, Little Grey in a field. Though they have never ridden before, they climb on his back and canter off into the woods for the day.

In one of *Ginn's Rescue Adventures, Shorty Again* by James Webster, two boys walking the dog along the beach disregard signs at a dangerous cave, hoping to find treasure. Instead of meeting with calamity, the boys become involved with a film crew and even find chocolate "gold". No lesson is learnt, save the importance of luck! Amazon's website for this book has links to the Ginn Literary Scheme described as the best KS1 and KS2 reading programmes for your primary school!

It is surprising how many references there are to hitch-hiking! In *Eight Children and a Truck* (by Anne-Cath Vestly), the "how to" details of Grandma hitching home seem unwise. The hero of the *Tim and Tobias* series has no qualms about riding with a strange truck-driver, nor is his friend Kevin a good example on the road. Showing off his new bicycle, in Book C1, "he slipped in and out among the cars riding as fast as he could".

Further dangerous ideas are given, in *Yellow Book 7 of One, Two, Three and Away* and in *Moon of Gomrath*, about children lighting fires in the woods. Jimmy, the owner of *T.R.Bear*, not only carries matches in his pocket but also a few bangers and a catapult and boasts, "I'm pretty good with it".

It is also important to mention here the power of "a dare". This was the trigger that compelled Frankie to jump out of a tall tree. On the *Island of the Strangers* it is a dare that leads Nora to stay there longer than she should. She boasts, "I was the only one not afraid to stay at the Spaniard's house in the dark and I was going to make sure they all knew it". Her action leads to deceit and requires a return visit to find her anorak. On this occasion she acts the hero, sliding between rocks to rescue the rival gang-leader. The danger is played down. The reader is constantly told Nora is not going to die. There is no sense of pain or ordeal, only the excitement of the helicopter rescue.

Since youngsters find it so hard to resist a dare, they need to be made aware of the dangers and to be given role-models with the strength of character to stand against peer pressure. Many will fear being labelled feeble if they do not respond to the challenge of Pamela Oldfield's *Spine Chillers*: "Read it if you dare!" Bernard Ashley's *All I Ever Ask* may actually dare the reader to watch horror films, even though they give the hero a real fright.

It takes great skill to tackle subjects which are likely to harm children without giving them an unduly high profile. In the third book of the *Oxford Junior Readers,* Roderick Hunt succeeds, in *The Red and White Scarf*, in warning of the dangers of losing one's temper and acting dangerously in defiance of the rules.

D3.0) Are distressing subjects dealt with sensitively?

Whilst we deplore the desensitising effect of too much horror, we must also have concern for those who suffer deep distress as they identify with victims of violence or tragedy. Fear attacks our security. Usually, children have not become hardened to the evils of the adult world, nor would we want them to be. The way in which pain and death are portrayed needs checking for suitability for a particular age-group and sensitivity of treatment.

Friends of Pine Street contains several references to death: Jon saw his father killed on the farm; Mr Crump ran away to sea when his mother died; the headmistress was fatally wounded when the roof fell in. The stark message that death is normal is almost callous, lacking compassion. No warning is given to the reader to prepare for a disaster. Harrowing comments about death only increase fear of the unknown. The hero's words from *On the Lion's Side*: "seeing what death did to people, and awful separation, and years of loneliness", hold little hope of grief healed. There is also a very blunt and unnecessary reference to his mother's miscarriage.

The theme of *The Night Swimmers*, by Betsy Byars, is centred on a family's reactions to their mother's death. The father's goal, to become a singing star, is an escape mechanism from the real issues. He does not help his children come to terms with bereavement. "He never interfered …Besides, if he asked Retta what was wrong she might tell him". Retta's assertive attitude regarding her rights, her hatred of her younger brothers and her dislike of anyone who challenges her protective role over them are all due to her mother's death, but will the young reader understand this? Is this a suitable angle for a work of junior fiction? When the young brothers misbehave and Roy nearly drowns, the author's message is: They did nothing wrong, for everyone goes trespassing. They should not feel guilty; their father was to blame!

Guilt comes naturally from a bad conscience, but is often a facet of grief too. It is not easily dispelled. If we deprive our children of the peace of knowing forgiveness, and the promise of eternal life through Jesus, then we give them less than the best. I cannot speak too highly of Doris Buchanan-Smith's *A Taste of Blackberries*. When the head-strong Jamie dies unexpectedly, his young friend must come to terms with the loss, the sense of guilt, the numbness, the self-pity. His emotional struggle is treated with honesty and integrity. The loving family relationships, the Christian burial and the natural reference to heaven have a healing effect. There is the reassurance of being able to laugh and play again and that Jamie would approve.

Death of people and of pets is by no means the only distressing subject for children. Other stressful circumstances include accidents and illness. For some youngsters in hospital, it would not be helpful to have recently read of witches on the wards, as in Terence Blacker's *In Stitches with Ms Wiz*. Nor is the description of Minty's trauma at her mother's car accident, in *Moondial,* likely to prepare readers to cope with a similar event.

Some of the Ahlbergs' tales refer to burglars, whose threat is enhanced by rather creepy illustrations which could be worrying to imaginative youngsters. Examples include *Master Money the Millionaire* and *The Vanishment of Thomas Tull*. It is so important for adults to be monitoring what their children are reading and to be prepared to give time to talk through the issues raised in order to give protection and reassurance.

Finally, it must be admitted that in any civilisation mankind is naturally war-like, defending territory, retaking ground from the enemy and meeting out punishment on those who thwart him. As the adrenaline flows, excitement as well as horror is felt in the heat of the violence. We are reminded in Ephesians 6:12 that the real struggle is not against human enemies but against the motivating sources of evil. Perhaps God has created us with aggressive instincts in order to be effective in the spiritual battle. If we honour a God whose justice is tempered with mercy, we will want to emulate his ways and teach our children not only fairness and just deserts, but also forgiveness and self-control.

If children's novels are to reflect life honestly, they have to embrace all its aspects, though in a careful and controlled way. Some conflict or distress may be necessary. A key question to be addressed is, "What attitudes are aroused in the reader?" In *Pangur Ban,* violence is portrayed as necessary though horrible. The reader suffers the pain of Arthmael's wounds, knowing his true identity. Just like the agony of Jesus' scourging, we are relieved that, with the outpouring of the Dolphin's blood, Finglass is saved from bondage and death.

This is obviously in a different category from the general and gratuitous aggression we have been concerned about in this chapter. We must also remember to question motives. Is the aggression used purely for excitement, for material gain, for power, or in self-defence? Even when the violence is carried out by the villains, their actions are not always punished, neither are their motives condemned.

As an action-packed thriller for older boys, I can recommend one of the *Hardy Boys Casefiles* – *Dead on Target*. Franklin W. Dixon has succeeded fairly well in delivering the violence with restraint, in rationed doses, without dwelling on the details. The story begins with Joe's girlfriend being blown up by a car bomb, but the reader is spared explicit horror: "The car, and Iola, had erupted in a ball of white-hot flame". Frank softens the blow: "She wouldn't have lasted a second".

The plot is convincing. We cheer on the heroes as they overcome terrorists, escape Houdini-style from the enemy, defuse a bomb and save the senator. It is all very clean-cut and fair-play. Joe even attempts to save the killer's life because otherwise "I'd be no better than you". We hear just "one incoherent yell" as he falls from the third storey. Frank observes that, "He lived by blood and he died by it".

We must also ask, "Who is receiving the violence? Is it the villain, an innocent victim, or even the hero?" Distress to the hero will be felt more keenly by the reader than that of a minor character and therefore needs more careful treatment. "Who is delivering the violence?" The heroes' actions will be powerful role-models.

In *Songs on the South Bank* by Chris Ashley, young Robert regrets his involvement with football hooliganism, though feeling brave and excited at first. He loathes the racial hatred, yet is scared to break free from the mindless mob. As he witnesses his granddad being knocked down in the street, he feels ashamed and realises he is not enjoying himself at all. The menacing atmosphere is achieved without horrific details.

The problem of violence is very much on our public agenda as people begin to wonder where we have gone wrong:

"Aggression, verbal bullying, overtly aggressive sexual gestures used in celebration by footballers and other games players, pornography, sexism, illegal drugs, alcohol and drunkenness, materialism and selfishness. Are these on the increase or am I just getting old?"

These are the words, not of a probation officer in an inner-city, but of the principal of a public school in Hertfordshire, as long ago as 1990 (quoting David Jewell's interview in *The Independent*). Has anything changed? In spite of the introduction of V-chip technology for blocking violence on the television, only a minority of parents use it! However, it behoves all those who care to expose the less obvious influences of poor role-models and confused values, even in picture-books, and to deal with the problem at the point at which attitudes are formed in the developing mind.

Recommended Books

For Younger Readers

Mr. Biff the Boxer   by Ahlberg.

Distress

Small Pig   by A.Lobel.

Not Anywhere House by D.Hendry.

Harry's Night Out by A.Pizer.

Better Move on Frog by R.Maris.

Mary Kate and the School Bus by H.Morgan.

Let's Go Home Little Bear by M.Waddell.

The Kite (Roundabouts) by Pat Belford.

Alice Alone by S.Isherwood.

Death

Wish You Were Here by C.Zolotow.

Laura's Granny by S.Bowen.

For Older Readers

Dead on Target by Dixon.

Songs on the South Bank by C.Ashley.

Distress

Quake by M.Hardcastle.

Different Dragons by J.Little.

Nothing Else Matters by P.St.John.

Tim's Knight by S.Isherwood.

Death

The Tanglewoods' Secret by P.St.John.

A Taste of Blackberries by D.Buchanan-Smith.

Chapter 9: <u>FAIRY TALE AND FANTASY</u>

"Let no-one deceive you with empty words…"   (Eph. 5:6)

E) Is fantasy used to widen the imagination in a helpful and inspirational way?

Fantasy is the essence of childhood. It is the stuff that dreams are made of, particularly day-dreams! In its widest sense, fantasy is what happens in the mind. It is nourished by imagery and the printed word and often finds an outlet in play. For *our* purposes, fantasy includes any story which is not realistic, though it may deal with real fundamental issues. Its symbolism provides a most valuable opportunity for teaching moral and spiritual attitudes and clarifying the deeper meaning of life.

Fantasy may have a dream-like quality; it may describe impossible situations and events; it probably features characters whom one would never meet in real life. Under this definition, we must embrace fairy stories, folk tales, myths, legends, allegory, fables and many other animal stories, as well as science-fiction and modern mystical works. Unfortunately, the latter often digress into the realms of the New Age and the occult. Let us first consider which aspects of fantasy we might endorse, before investigating the ways in which modern writers have abused this genre.

The traditional folk or fairy tale is part of our heritage and has always been characterised by certain distinguishing features. Central to the plot there might well be a royal family with two or three sons, the youngest symbolising humility and often displaying such virtues as integrity, courage and wisdom.

Alternatively, the hero might be a woodcutter, or some other lowly but honest person, typically kind and diligent. He would often embark on a quest or set out to seek his fortune, to decide who is the most faithful, or who should win the princess's hand. There was often a forest, which represented the great wide world, and perhaps a mountain, as an obstacle which must be overcome. There would normally be close family relationships unless affected by unusual circumstances such as a second marriage!

There would be a number of fabulous characters present, each clearly aligned with either good or evil. Amongst the friendly ones would be fairies, elves, pixies, dwarfs, gnomes, nymphs, genies or talking animals. From Ruskin Bond's *Tales and Legends from India,* we learn that fairies are a derivation of the peris of Persian folklore who were beautiful sprites. Later they were regarded as delicate and gentle, "helping the pure in heart to find their way to heaven". Bond also informs us that dryads, whom we meet in the *Narnia* series, were woodland gods.

These definitions reflect heathen beliefs. Christians believe the only way to heaven is through Jesus who saves us and makes us worthy (Acts 4:12, Romans 3:22). Therefore in the Christianised world, fairies have become "nice nonsense", as Winkie Pratney calls it. Though, like nymphs, they may have pagan origins, we do not now consider them to be real. They support, rather than conflict with, Christian values.

C.S.Lewis certainly did not intend his naiads and dryads to represent pagan power. In *The Lion, the Witch and the Wardrobe*, he refers to them as Tree-Women and Well-Women who acknowledge the lordship of Aslan and form part of his great company. They represent the water and the woods personified (cf. Romans 8:19). Similarly in *Prince Caspian*, Lewis regards Bacchus merely as a mythical creature playing the part of master of ceremonies at the celebration of Aslan's victory, whilst the river god appeals to the Lion for deliverance from his chains.

Traditionally, those on the enemy's side would include the wicked witch or wizard, ogres, giants, dragons, monsters and goblins. There were also some like trolls and leprechauns who should be treated with suspicion in view of their mischief and unreliability.

One could be sure that goodness would be rewarded and evil receive its just deserts. To achieve this there would be the suggestion of a benevolent but invisible power, perhaps controlling amazing happenings, or providing gifts through a fantasy agent for the benefit of the hero, probably symbolising the help of the omnipresent God at a much deeper level.

Though termed "fairy stories", there is often no sign of the little people in these traditional tales, yet enchantment abounds. However, this magic is employed merely to emphasise the element of fantasy. We deny the richness of the English language when we limit our vocabulary and use one word for many concepts. The word "magic" is an obvious example. It has a whole gamut of meanings, from children's party entertainment to black magic in satanic ritual.

Some parents would seek to shield their children from all magic. They believe that even conjuring and sleight of hand are a form of deception which in itself is harmful. We must respect that position. In the main though, I feel Christians would agree that such tricks have nothing to do with the supernatural and therefore fall into a different category.

There is another distinct use of the term "magic". It satisfies a longing to understand "the unexplained". To a child, much of the world around him is awesome, bewildering, beyond his comprehension. In *The Secret Garden*, the classic by Frances Hodgson Burnett, Colin marvels that everything is made out of magic. He means that which he cannot understand because of its specialness. His wonder leads him to praise God. Many things appear to happen as if "by magic". Generations of story-tellers have used this convention to capture the mystery of life, perhaps to avoid religious or philosophical explanations that would be too deep or complex, out of place in a child's book and better removed to the fantastic or allegorical plane.

In *Beauty and the Beast* (by de Villeneuve) and *The Frog Prince* (Grimm Brothers) the *mechanics* of changing into a prince are effected "by magic", whilst the reader is persuaded that it is *love* that transforms people and restores them to fullness of life. Evil spells are broken, not by more spells, but by virtue, thus supporting the message that good overcomes evil. Such a change in a person may result from tapping his own inner resources. In *The King's Choice (Myths and Legends* by R.Hunt), each of three princes must drink a magic potion to decide the most suitable heir to the throne. Its effect is to exaggerate their natural qualities, thus making the choice more obvious.

Magic as a convention may be used to effect a change of circumstances as a result of virtuous behaviour. To emphasise the lesson that unselfishness will be rewarded, Salozan's sovereign doubles when used to help others, but is worth only half as much when he spends it on himself *(Salozan and the Golden Sovereign* by E.S.Bradburne, *Gold and Silver* reading scheme).

Another acceptable use of magic is as a device to breach the limitations of a child's world, either to render him invisible, or as a vehicle into another dimension of time and space, one which would normally be impossible to attain. It answers the wish, "If only I could...". "If only I were grown-up and ruled my own kingdom" is fulfilled in the *Narnia* series. In *Gold Book 4 (Gold and Silver series)*, the aspiration to fly up to the stars is realised with the help of *The Magic Horse.* Such flights of fantasy develop the imagination positively without endangering the reader in any way.

Characteristic of traditional fantasy is the distancing of the events from the reader into another realm, though retaining acceptable values and the confidence that God still reigns. The reader knows by the presence of fantasy-type characters, strange circumstances, or the use of unfamiliar vocabulary, such as swine-herds, kingdoms, suitors, sovereigns, or even aliens, that a step has been taken out of the mundane and into the extra-ordinary. This allows fewer restrictions and greater possibilities for the plot. Heroes may even be adult, thus giving insight into the behaviour of mature people.

The fantasy villain is probably more repulsive than one who is human, thus persuading the reader to reject him. Evil actions committed in a fantasy realm, wolves or ogres gobbling up girls and boys, imprisonment in tall towers, are unlikely to be copied by the reader owing to lack of inclination or opportunity! Violent and evil elements being removed from the child's familiar world may not be so alarming, except for the very young or sensitive. The wicked witch is less terrifying in a candy cottage, or in Narnia, than when too close for comfort in a bedroom or kitchen. C.S. Lewis has said:

"In fairy tales, side by side with the terrible figures, we find the comforters and protectors, the radiant ones. It would be nice if no little boy in bed, hearing or thinking he hears a sound, was ever at all frightened, but if he *is* going to be frightened I think it better that he should think of giants and dragons than merely burglars. And I think St.George, or any bright champion in armour, is a better comfort than the idea of the police."

Yet paradoxically, fantasy feeds the mind with very powerful imagery, conveying truth with more impact perhaps than the more obvious type of plot. We expect to find in folk tales a specific lesson to be learned or a warning to be heeded. So Perrault wrote *Little Red Ridinghood* in order to warn unsuspecting girls at court of the "wolves" that surrounded them, whilst the famous fable of *The Hare and the Tortoise* by Jean de la Fontaine teaches us not to boast or be complacent.

The quest is the convention expressing the search for the meaning and purpose of life, giving a vision beyond oneself. Such journeys teach perseverance and faithfulness, and typify this genre which G.K.Chesterton called "spiritual explorations". Because fantasy is removed from reality it tends to bring revelation regarding the motivating powers behind the action, so bringing a spiritual dimension to the story.

Perrault's work abounds in Christian symbolism. In the much-loved *Puss in Boots,* a poor miller dies leaving his mill, a donkey and a cat to his three sons. The youngest son feels hard done by when left with the cat, but buys him a pair of boots and agrees to accept his help. The boy, following the cat's plan, enters the river as though drowning and reappears as a new person, the Marquis of Carabas. Puss gains favour for his master from the King, claims princely clothes and land, and finally ousts the ogre from his castle. The boy, in grateful wonderment, receives these provisions and marries the princess. Here in picture language we see the Gospel: baptism, new royal status and acceptance with God, and the reclaiming of the devil's ground.

Elizabeth Cook is the author of *The Ordinary and the Fabulous (an Introduction to Myths, Legends and Fairy-Tales for Teachers and Story-Tellers).* She asserts that modern versions have distorted Perrault's *Cinderella,* presenting it as shallow wish-fulfilment when really it is a story about "Trial, Recognition and Judgement". Cinderella is "her father's true heir, and is born to be a queen. Her place in the family is usurped by the Proud Sisters, they try to prevent her from entering the contest by which the right to the kingdom is to be decided". This of course holds Christian imagery. Magic is used only as a device to strip away "the disguise that conceals the soul". The heroine bears her trial like a princess, with dignity, "no self-pity and *no wishing*". Cook argues that new translations have turned her into a cry-baby, a mere child, in no way fit for a throne!

Stories in which the weak and humble battle against great difficulties and triumph over evil reflect the amazing paradox, that a helpless baby born in a stable was destined to defeat Satan and save the world. Christian writers past and present have used the opportunities that fantasy affords to underline the fundamental truths of the Christian faith. Jesus himself used picture language as he taught in parables, intending his listeners to think carefully and see beyond the obvious.

Of course, Jesus never used the word "magic", but neither do many folk tales either, though they rely on the miraculous to convey the mystery and greatness of God and his world. It is important for *us* too, as parents and teachers, not to equate God's awesome power with magic, but to clarify what is pure fantasy, what is real and what is supernatural. Fairy tale magic *is* different from that used in occult activity, the dangers of which are the subject of the next chapter. It is important to be clear what the differences are and to explain them to our children as soon as they are old enough to understand.

Some folk tales make the point that real magic is uncomfortable, unpredictable and frightening. Stories like *The Sorcerer's Apprentice* and *The Magic Porridge Pot*, in which the hero cannot stop the spell, or regrets his wish having been granted, give a valuable warning. In fact, Elizabeth Cook reveals that "wish-come-true" stories traditionally come to a sticky end, e.g. *King Midas* and *Why the Sea is Salt* (quoting form *The Ordinary and the Fabulous*).

The fact that the great and powerful do not always win, holds great appeal for children who readily identify with the youngest, the weakest, the underestimated hero. The frustrations of being small and feeling powerless and insignificant in a grown-ups' world are eased by a make-believe scenario where little old Mrs Pepperpot (*Mrs Pepperpot's Busy Day* by Alf Proysen) overcomes the problems of being reduced in size for a day. With great ingenuity she manages to wash clothes and cook supper for a husband who never realises the effort she has made. Children warm to characters smaller than themselves and are more fascinated by the ladybird's eye-view than that of the giant.

This is why the fairy folk hold such fascination. These tiny figures, which are not real but seem so, represent freedom from restriction and a measure of power. Some authors have used imaginary friends, or toys that come to life, like *Miss Happiness and Miss Flower* by Rumer Godden, to serve the same purpose. These companions provide security, rather like Jesus the unseen friend, and also an opportunity for the active imagination to expand in the child's own world. How much better it is to encourage these harmless secrets than the sort that put up barriers against parents and lead to furtive behaviour.

Having defined our expectations, we are better equipped to decide what our requirements of modern fantasy are, and to discern whether a particular story succeeds or fails. Many of the questions already asked in sections A - D will be relevant and useful in our assessment.

E1.0) In modern fantasy, do acceptable values still hold?

Fairy tales are still being written; many modern writers are copying the tried and tested traditional style which is so attractive to children. Sara and Stephen Corrin, well-known for their collections of short stories, suggest in their introduction to *The Puffin Book of Modern Fairy Stories* that both the old and new fairy tales create a world which the reader has to take seriously − "a secondary world with its *own laws* of logic and justice … the domain of magic and enchantment". (My italics).

I reiterate the warning that fantasy realms are fraught with danger if alternative deities hold sway, or if the rules and alignments have been changed. Children seek, subconsciously, to interpret the world around them. Just as fantasy is a powerful medium through which to convey truth, it may also promote lies. What is being taught in modern fantasy? Let us examine three stories from a collection of folk-tales by Ann Lawrence − *There and Back Again*. Do we see exemplary models in her heroes?

Mossy Coat treats her elderly suitor with contempt, using him to obtain beautiful dresses by false pretences, then disappearing to London to dazzle the prince whom she eventually marries in circumstances not unlike those of Cinderella. In *The Green Man of Knowledge*, Jack is lazy, dishonest, forgetful of instructions, and gambles his money away. He achieves his ambition to make his fortune, but when he is cornered into marriage one wonders, given his personality, how long it will last!

In *The Three Feathers*, the youngest of three sons has no desire for the throne, in other words, no aspirations to a noble calling. His motivation for marrying the enchanted frog's reptilian daughter is not one of selfless love and compassion, but to escape the responsibility of kingship! There is no message of courage or discipline being rewarded, only that life is unfair: he becomes king without really trying. Christian values are being overturned; the undeserving hero wins the prize.

One senses a certain cynicism in this tongue-in-cheek treatment which leaves a bad taste. E.Nesbit's *The Charmed Life (Puffin Book of Modern Fairy Stories)* is really a parody of the traditional moral tale which will be lost on most children. The king fails in the royal business and becomes instead Rex Bloomsbury, lift-maker. The prince is given a charmed life as a baby which he hides behind a brick in the wall! No contest between good and evil, no quest and no particularly honourable hero, rather this is a romantic study on class distinction. The prince finally wins his princess in disguise!

Andrew Lang, the great collector of fairy stories, translated from foreign sources and at the end of the 19th century wrote down material hitherto passed on only by word of mouth (*The Coloured Fairy Books*). He set a good example in recording only decent versions with nothing that might offend modesty. It is startling therefore to meet indelicacy in modern tales which seems out of character. In Diana Ross's *The Young Man with Music in his Fingers*, the hero seeking his fortune is rewarded for his kindness and marries the princess. What a surprise then, to be confronted by a full-page picture of the Sea-Maiden rising naked out of the water, her female figure enhanced, rather than covered, by her hair.

Since *The Robber's Daughter* is written by a Swedish author, Astrid Lindgren, we might expect some liberality! Explicit illustrations of nudity portray not only breast-feeding but twelve male robbers washing in the snow – no modesty here. This is a fascinating story with a medieval flavour. The fantasy element is reinforced by the goblin folk and menacing harpies. In such a setting it hardly seems strange that Kirsty should venture alone in the forest to learn its dangers and overcome her fears, since in *this* case the forest is her world. After a loving and open relationship with her parents we see disillusionment and the loosening of ties.

Coming to terms with suspicion, jealousy and quarrels, her friendship with Burl blossoms and though they live together in a cave, the complete absence of sexual innuendo renders the situation acceptable. It also underlines their innocence. They reject their parents' way of life and determine to live honestly. Unfortunately, intertwined with this positive message is the insinuation that the children are "much wiser" than their parents. Of course this is not usually so. The Christian way is for parents to pass on wisdom and truth to the next generation.

1.1) Does symbolism lead the reader into spiritual truth or confusion?

"But you, O God, are my King from of old; you bring salvation upon the earth.

… you broke the heads of the monster in the waters.

 It was you who crushed the heads of Leviathan …"   (Psalm 74:12-14).

As a result of standing convention on its head, those fabulous figures which traditionally represented evil are now often portrayed as reformed characters. Take dragons, for instance, equated with serpents in the Bible and symbolic of Satan. In Revelation 20 we see the angel locking the hideous Dragon away to keep him from deceiving the nations. His ultimate fate is to be thrown into a lake of sulphur. Whether you interpret this literally or otherwise, the meaning is clear.

Even so, we find a plethora of sweet, "misunderstood" dragons in children's books. We sympathise with *Bella's Dragon* (by Chris Powling) who is lonely. She installs him in the boiler-room to keep the school warm. Titles of a similar ilk include Mary Hoffman's *Beware Princess*, Cresswell's *Dragon Ride* and Brenda Smith's *Charlie Dragon* which is friendly, yet not averse to gobbling up princesses!

Kaye Umansky follows suit with her *Big Iggy*. As Large Lizzie warns her poor little offspring, "It's bad manners to eat a princess", readers are reassured. They are invited to identify with this dragon family who, after cleaning their fangs enjoy a bedtime lullaby: ---

"You'll find all the friendship you crave

In the wonderful Land of the Dragon.

We'll listen and learn to be wise …

To be proud of our wings

And all Dragonish things."

As Iggy ventures into the Wide World he discovers that adults expect him to be bad. However, the wise little princess who befriends him knows better! She is the one who brings freedom to both the dragon *and* the knight, but Iggy is hailed as the hero, the saviour who disposes of the villain in a nettle bed!

Ann Ruffell speaks out admirably against greed and materialism in *Dragon Earth*, yet again as we recognise ourselves in this humanised beast we soften towards him; our outrage against this monster is quenched. If greed, like other sins, is a temptation Satan puts in our way, then what a nonsense to reject greed, whilst embracing the dragon! St.James' Epistle still urges us to "Resist the devil and he will flee from you" (James 4:7), but sadly the seriousness of the battle is being lost.

Kenneth Grahame's *Reluctant Dragon*, originally published in 1898, might well have been speaking a prophetic warning to the church, supposed to be Christian soldiers, but who have settled down into a cosy compromise with the devil (2Tim.3:5). A Boy (representing worldly influence?) persuades St.George (the church?) and the dragon (the devil?) to come to an arrangement – a show fight to keep everyone content. St.George is happy because "he hadn't had to kill anybody; for he didn't really like killing…" and the dragon is happy: "he had won popularity and a sure footing in society". Is it not significant that this story has been resurrected *at this time*? Joining the ranks of many other harmless dragons now in vogue, its satirical thrust has lost its cutting edge. It now blends well with current New Age concepts of peace with all and avoidance of confrontation.

Other kinds of monsters have also been robbed of their ferocity, like the polite one in *The Worm and the Toffee-Nosed Princess* by Eva Ibbotson, and the timid one in McCullagh's *The Little Monster* who is afraid of mice. The message here is: all is relative. More acceptable are the stegosaurus-type monsters found in *Thingnapped* by Robin Klein, and *Gumdrop and the Monster* by Val Biro which do not carry the same symbolism. These are really "what if" stories. They pose the question, "What would happen if dinosaurs were family pets?!"

Ruth Manning-Sanders, in her collection of tales from around the world, *A Book of Ogres and Trolls,* defines ogres as traditionally wicked, cruel and treacherous. It seems unwise therefore to publish in Magnet picture-book format *Zeralda's Ogre* (T.Ungerer) in which a girl befriends a lonely giant, accompanies him to his castle and eventually marries him! It seems giants too have changed sides.

A six-year-old once came to me with her reading book, McCullagh's *In the Castle.* She questioned me about one of the pictures.

"Are giants supposed to be nasty?" she queried.

I affirmed that they are.

With a puzzled frown she said, "But this one looks kind!"

Here is evidence of a child attempting to clarify truth but receiving confusion.

The message that love transforms evil is a false one. On the cross, Jesus *disarmed* the Devil, and so we see love overcoming the *power* of evil over people's lives, as illustrated by *Beauty and the Beast*. However, fantasy ogres by their very size symbolise the very source of evil which is beyond redemption. In fact, there were once real giants whose origin is recorded in Genesis 6. There we read that giants were not truly human, but born of demonic fathers (fallen angels like Satan himself) and human mothers. They were the men of renown in the early myths (Gen.6:4). According to Bible teacher Roger Price, their purpose was to pollute humanity, thus thwarting God's plans for the coming Messiah. God ensured that they were all wiped out by the end of King David's reign, the most notorious being Goliath. Their Satanic origin was not to be tolerated.

So what must children believe when Leeson persuades them that *The Reversible Giant* has repented? The obligation to kill him has been removed. Robin announces, "Don't be afraid. The giant is your friend!" It is my belief that dragons and monsters, and witches and wizards which we will look at in detail in chapter 10, have been ameliorated not to protect children from horror or the unpleasant facts of life, for there are plenty of other examples of these, but in order to deny that they are at all evil, and to deceive youngsters into believing they are good and helpful, or at least just human like us. They no longer fulfil their function in fantasy.

Ngaio Malcolm links the problem with horror stories shorn of moral values. She once wrote an article for the Librarians' Christian Fellowship entitled *A Great Gulf Fixed?* which is available to read on-line. In it she describes new fantasy stories as "emaciated versions" designed "to make sure that no child will ever again be frightened by wicked witches, man-eating giants or cunning wolves" because "there is really no evil to fight… they grow up unable to choose the good and reject the evil because they scarcely know the difference and the result is real monsters – murderers, rapists and child abusers – who cannot feel guilt because the whole concept of right and wrong is foreign to them". She maintains that this is "another manifestation of the humanist attempt to abolish absolutes".

If there is no evil and everyone is good, the nasty characters – werewolves, demons, vampires – must be pure fantasy, rather than symbolic of real powers. Therefore we can enjoy horror! This is the deception and confusion being sown amongst our children.

1.2) Does fantasy clarify reality – or is it gratuitous escapism?

Because fantasy must be extra-ordinary by definition, it often takes place in an imaginary setting, perhaps with the semblance of the possible, the vaguely European Ruritania, or *Rob's Place*, the fantasy island across the lake, or maybe an entirely different world like Narnia or *Alice in Wonderland*. Wherever the situation, it must measure up to our criteria. What does the story teach regarding insights on life? Does it give suitable role-models for personal relationships, or for coping with difficulties?

Gilbert Adair has written a new Alice book in the traditional style of Lewis Carroll − *Alice Through the Needle's Eye*. It need not worry us that the heroine explores alone, for the fantasy element has been established: she has slipped through the eye of a needle and no-one would expect her parents to follow! Adair plays on words and uses the alphabet as his theme. We sense his Christian sympathies when he lists faith, freedom and forgiveness as good things beginning with F, as opposed to fear and falsehood which are bad. He uses this medium of the metaphorical to explain curious phrases like *running* a temperature and *jumping* to conclusions, and how, having arrived *elsewhere*, you are now *here*!

This ingenious book is great fun and its excitement does not depend on coarse language, violence or occult content. It can be done! However, in the light of the all too frequent tragedies associated with railway lines, due either to vandalism or misadventure, I was surprised to find the usually sensible Alice complying with Grampus' idiotic ambition to be tied to the track and rescued just in the nick of time! It is also a rather dangerous idea to carry a needle in one's pocket. Perhaps the fact that she pricks her finger on waking serves as a warning.

Though modern fantasy is often lacking in spiritual truths, it is sometimes used as a vehicle for imparting general knowledge. In *Wings* by Terry Pratchett, the diminutive nomes receive explanatory information about the humans' world from The Thing, a sort of computerised guide. At the same time young readers learn about density of air, space-flight and other scientific facts without the tedium of the text-book. Similarly, Lindgren's strange orphan *Pippi Longstocking*, though capable of amazing feats, needs everything explained to her.

However, some stories appear to *promote* the benefits of the fantasy world for its own sake. Rob creates a Paradise Island (*Rob's Place*) where he can escape the pressures of a broken home. What at first seems harmlessly exciting begins to take over Rob's mind as Perilous Island.

In *Cry of a Seagull*, it is Rose who finds it difficult to shake off her other existence. This fictional situation is based on the fact that children do waver between the land of daydreams and the real world. We need not worry if they occasionally slip into fairyland, or venture to the limit of their own imagination, but if that secret world has been invaded by violent or occultic images, and has opened doors that should have remained locked, then much harm may be done.

The great danger of the role-playing adventure books is that youngsters are sucked into an alternative scenario, more of a nightmare than a daydream, and encouraged to stay there! Brennan's *Monster Horrorshow* is introduced as a "magical world of nightmare … you live or die for days, weeks, months, years … takes place in your head … first you learn to become a were wizard". This is very similar to the rules of the adventure game/books *Dungeons and Dragons* which urge the players to keep their own character from one game to the next, even when moving to a new neighbourhood. Rather than being removed from real life, *this* fantasy clings to the reader, encompassing him in the action; it no longer has the safety barriers in place; it is too close to ignore. It demands total involvement which can easily grow into addiction.

A friend told me of her son's experience. At the age of ten he began spending his pocket money on *Jackson and Livingstone Fighting Fantasies* until he had acquired a stack of them. At the same time he became increasingly withdrawn, reading them in his room for hours on end. As his school work deteriorated and bad behaviour increased his teachers became worried and sought an interview with his mother who, being already concerned about the books, came home and destroyed them. Her son never mentioned it, never asked about the books. He gradually returned to normal behaviour and gained many friends. His mother said, "It was as though the books had a hold over him while they were in the house. Once they were gone they had no more influence".

The problem is that children enjoy these multi-option adventures which are written by very skilful authors who know what appeals. There *are* good ones available, so it is worth taking the trouble to sift through the selection, but do not be deceived. *Hijacked* by R.Brightfield, for the ten plus age-group, gives the impression from its illustrations that it comes from the Enid Blyton mould. However, each episode culminates in a grisly death − unless you win! To be gassed, thrown out of a helicopter or left to drown in a water-filled chamber are a few of the possibilities!

It is the dreamlike quality of *Spellhorn* that lends legitimacy to the dual life. Laura rejects the opportunity to return to her family, hankering after an older and better place, yet later realises it is possible to live in both worlds. Rather than clarify reality, the Wilderness itself, where the Unicorn is the saviour, becomes real. Stated another way, the Fraggles (*Red and the Pumpkins*), trying to rescue Red from her nightmare, know its potential power: "If a dream was dreamed hard enough and long enough it could come true".

Dreams are a fascinating area for writers to explore. They give a valid excuse for incredible tales and are all very well as long as the criteria apply. In *Gumdrop and the Secret Switches,* Val Biro has no need to resort to magic to cause the veteran car to drive over water, fly in the sky and win the race. Finally facing the disaster of an empty petrol-tank we learn it is only a dream!

Warning bells sound when stories encourage children to try voluntarily to return to the dream state. This verges on transcendental meditation and occult practice. Some authors seem to use the ethereal medium of fantasy to express the subconscious mind, which easily slips into the surrealist mode. Take for example *Meal One*. Helbert plants a plum-stone under the bed. It grows as soon as he summons it, filling the house, invading the kitchen and eating his breakfast, which is referred to as "meal one" – why? To make it more unreal?

There is certainly a surrealist atmosphere surrounding the *Iron Man* which begins: "Where had he come from? Nobody knows." He appears on a cliff-edge and throws himself over for no apparent reason, his body parts lying strewn across the beach. Having miraculously but gruesomely restored himself, he disappears into the sea. Living on a diet of metal, it is said that he is growing rusty owing to all the barbed wire he has eaten. Any child could tell you it is because he spends so much of his time under either earth or sea! One can almost be convinced by the absurdities in these stories unless one checks and takes stock, like Alice who says, "What nonsense we are talking!"

Gilbert Adair brings us back to the norm as a standard by which to measure, in order to reject the neurotic and idiotic. If, through nonsense fantasy, an author is able to expose the quirks and paradoxes of life and laugh at its incongruities, if he urges children to question double standards, to uphold integrity and reject pretence, if he inspires them to wonder at life and develop enquiring minds, then he has achieved an admirable purpose.

However, to set before the young reader a "what if" story like *Conrad the Factory-Made Boy* seems merely to sow the seeds of dissension. It asks, "What would happen if children were required to be naughty rather than good?" This is a scenario which would not succeed, but appears to here by breaking all the rules. It plants the idea, which grows into a conviction, that children might be wiser than their parents. This unhelpful message does not clarify life but contributes to a destabilising of the family and rebellion against the status quo.

On a more encouraging note, I must mention two books which are worthy of praise. Gale Haley's *Birdsong* is a beautifully illustrated fairy tale in the old style. The orphaned heroine's love for the birds compels her, in spite of personal danger, to free the birds from the greedy bird-catcher. They in turn rescue her and whisk her away to their secret kingdom. A magic feather is used as a device to bring about her special empathy with her feathered friends.

Quentin Blake's is the story of *Patrick* who gives his last silver coin for an old violin which brings colour and excitement into people's lives. He plays for a poorly tinker, bringing him health and happiness again. Reminiscent of the parable of the pearl of great price (Mat.13:45), the theme is one of true riches which are more valuable than any money.

E2.0) Does our choice of fantasy fiction include adequate variety?

Whereas in the past fantasy has been synonymous with fairy tale, more recently there has been a danger of concentrating too heavily on witches and the supernatural as an aid to the imagination. It would be good to see a greater variety on the shelves of children's libraries. There are many other avenues which could be safely explored, though even these have their pitfalls.

Animal stories are particularly successful and present fewer problems than most types of modern fiction! Their pages rarely contain bad language, immorality, violence or the occult. Animals are not bound by the limitations of childhood; they grow to maturity whilst retaining their vulnerability and offer their experience to the world. Even the night may be explored by young readers through the eyes of nocturnal creatures. Indeed, if these tales hold no other message, they usually give insight into animal behaviour and encourage a concern for their welfare. In addition, they often help us to recognise our own faults and foibles in a way that gently pricks the conscience.

The *Rats of Nimh* display great courage and perseverance as they help one another against their common enemies, the Cat and Man. *Pangur Ban the White Cat* underlines the truth that mankind depends on the help of animals; their lives are inextricably interdependent (compare Genesis 9:3&9 and Romans 8:19-21). Niall and the Cat share the guilt of their friend's death, and a common purpose to make amends.

Dick King-Smith sets his *Mouse Butcher* at a time in the future when all the humans have left, for some reason, and the cats have taken on the names and personalities of their previous owners. Tom Plug, the courageous hero, is a clever hunter in love with the colonel's daughter. Great Mog, bitter and twisted, jealously vows to kill Tom. He snarls, "Damn you Creep", to his lackey, but since he epitomises evil one should not be surprised! Ecclesiastes, the vicar's cat, quotes scripture most appropriately and is certain of the downfall of the devil. In an exciting climax Tom and Mog fight it out, without resorting to horrific details, at the top of the clock-tower. The vicar's trust, that help will come from on high, is rewarded and as lightening strikes they thank heaven for their deliverance!

Penelope Lively's *The Voyage of the QV66* also takes place in the future, after another Great Flood (see Genesis 9:11). In this case six animals set forth on a quest to discover the true identity of Stanley. *They* also have one among them who frequently quotes Scripture, though the cathedral Pigeon whose verses are not always so apt is often ignored. On sighting Pansy the Cat blown away with a balloon, he cries, "Rejoice with me for I have found my sheep which was lost". The canine narrator comments, "We told him to shut up and tell us which way to go".

The voyagers encounter unfriendly animals which are becoming more like humans. The rooks bully the Parrot and try to peck out its eyes because it is "different". The police dogs unjustly imprison Freda the Cow. Is this a political message? Arriving at their destination, London Zoo, Stanley meets with disillusionment. His fellow monkeys are lording it over everyone, forming useless committees of self-styled experts who know nothing. Surely this is a cynical comment on society!

Most weird of all is the ceremony at Stonehenge where creatures are offering Pansy as a sacrifice on a stone altar to ensure the sun continues to rise. Does this imply that animals evolving into humans would practise primeval religion? Who would expect such an innocent cover to conceal animal sacrifice − offered by animals? Consider the implications! Though not condoned, the event is portrayed as misguided rather than evil. Contrast this with the attempted sacrifice of Sarah, her wrists tied to two pillars, to appease the witch in Houghton's *Hagbane's Doom*. The wizards are very definitely identified with evil and their actions recognised as such.

Some fairy stories have developed from myth and legend which have a measure of truth, pointing back in time to the sustaining hand of God. Others say more about pagan beliefs with their gods and goddesses. These would be better suited to the classics student or the history class. If such stories *are* chosen for youngsters, great care is needed, as seen in chapter two.

Whilst 8-11's are attracted by the great heroes of old, often the names are too difficult to pronounce, the style too boring, the plot too intricate, the symbolism too deep, and the message too adult to hold interest. Drastic adaptation is often unsatisfactory to the literary experts and purists. St. Paul wisely warned: "Have nothing to do with godless myths and old wives' tales" (1 Tim. 4:7).

Long Ago and Yesterday (Book 6 of *Through the Rainbow* series, Bradburne) is typical of such collections which comprise a confusing mixture of beliefs. St.Francis, who commands the wolf in the name of Jesus Christ to do no harm, rubs shoulders with Demeter, about whom it is said: "Once upon a time… everything was in the care of the Mother of the Earth"; the victory of the Greeks by cunning deceit in the Trojan War vies for attention with the selflessness of missionary Gladys Aylward.

On the other hand, children of this age-group are prone to hero worship. The examples of bravery set by King Arthur's Knights or St. George facing difficulties alone but reaching their goal *are* attractive and hold particular appeal to a child lacking security, perhaps in a one-parent family. Such heroes are a better inspiration than a story which sets out to prove that a lone parent situation is normal or adequate. There is a definite need, therefore, for Christian writers to select those legends which hold worthwhile values and to retell them with sensitivity both to the original flavour and to the needs of the readership. This calls for a blend of spiritual discernment with literary skill.

Historical themes offer plenty of scope for the imagination, the distance from reality being a matter of time rather than space. Time has a mystery of its own, but in the attempt to capture this in story form there has been a tendency to link the pure fantasy of time-travel with some ghostly kind of Other Worldliness. To equate the two is deceptive and gives credence to the practice of contacting the spirits of the dead.

At the time of its publication, *Moondial* was described in a Puffin catalogue as "a tense mystery with shifts in time made possible by the sundial Minty finds … journeying back into the past she meets two children". Such a description glosses over the strongly occult atmosphere of this book which begins: "Even before she came to Belton, Minty Cane had known that she was a witch, or something very like it".

Alternatively, Philippa Pearce makes it clear that *Tom's Midnight Garden* is *not* about ghosts, but is a study on the mystery of time. Events happen only when the clock strikes thirteen – a fantasy time. Can time stand still? No, Hatty grows older, yet this story touches on eternity where there are no limits any more. We sense the assurance of Christian truth here, with good examples of responsible attitudes, promises kept, apologies given and the relief felt in doing the right thing.

Whilst Silverberg's *Project Pendulum* swings back and forth between the future and the pre-historic age with all the "hi-tec" jargon of 2016, *Wings* is a more humorous rendering of science-fiction, featuring the four-inch "nomes" of Terry Pratchett's active imagination. These little aliens, seeking to return from whence they came, are able in true fantasy fashion to overcome all the obstacles of smallness, even controlling their own space-ship. In this futuristic comedy, religious symbolism is still apparent. Among the nomes we find Gurder, the believer (in Arnold Bros who created his world), Angalo the agnostic and Masklin the scientist.

We must delve beneath the surface to discover the author's intent. A touch of cynicism is evident, though more towards religion than Christianity, but I wonder how youngsters would interpret this. Angalo insists, "Blind faith never works", and whilst the Bible states that "faith is … being certain of what we do not see" (Hebrews 11:1), Christians may feel that they have some *proof*, in Jesus Christ, to support their trust in God. Gurder experiences disillusionment when the deified Richard Arnold turns out to be human after all, but this has a wider connotation than the merely religious. Gurder *is* concerned about the truth. He says, "I just want to make sense of life". When the rest of his tribe sails away into the skies he selflessly stays behind for the sake of those yet unreached: "Someone ought to tell them about the ship coming back… about what's really true".

In contrast, Douglas Hill's *Galactic Warlord* is at first glance a typical battle between goodness and the devil. The Warlord is described as "all humanity's enemy" with the intention of "wrecking the galaxy with warfare and ruling over its ruins". The hero Kiell decries self-interest, prejudice, deceit and murder, yet one suspects it is more for social reasons than moral. Kiell is a mercenary, and proud of his fighting skills, but his motive is revenge. "All this fury, all this vengeful hatred followed into and through the blow" delivered to the enemy. The spiritual battle between good and evil should be a matter of justice and judgement, not hate and revenge. Significantly, this book further departs from Christian principles when Kiell, who has been protected and revitalised by the Overseers, refuses their lordship, preferring to trust in his own power.

Product of the 22nd century, Sophie, *An Ash-Blond Witch*, arrives in the conservation pocket of Urstwhile where Prudence who is "very religious and good" disapproves of Dorcas the local witch, "a real professional", and would like her burnt at the stake. Many inhabitants doubt there is life beyond the kingdom, which is another way of saying there *is* more to life than the obvious. Lillington suggests that witchcraft is a primitive form of science and that it is Prudence's ignorance of this technology which causes her intolerance! Finally, the influential Sophie decides that superstition must be true, even witches, devils, love and God. Dorcas is taken into the modern world to introduce witchcraft there. The cover blurb describes this book as "a delightful comedy".

Clearly, authors of many types of fantasy have recognised that theirs is an excellent medium for delivering messages of a supernatural kind, whether Christian or otherwise. There is a fine line between the traditionally spiritual nature of fantasy, and the modern trend towards the occult. In drawing this chapter to a close I would like to emphasise two points.

First it is important to consider whether a fantasy novel inspires the reader for good or ill, outward into life, or inward into a secret world, what *could* be termed "altered planes of consciousness". Proverb 28 says: "The one who chases fantasies will have his fill of poverty". It is preferable that fictional friends do not intentionally seek the fantasy world, but rather that it "just happens", as in *Prince Caspian* when Lucy and Edmund are whisked off the station-platform and arrive, to their great surprise, in Narnia. Similarly, in *Hagbane's Doom* the children arrive in the Great Forest as the outcome of innocent exploration.

We must also ask ourselves, "What kind of magic is being used?" Is it that which facilitates the fantasy element, or is it sought for its own sake as a new source of power? Is it in fact an introduction to the occult?

Further Recommended Titles

For Younger Readers

Jeremiah in the Dark Woods by Ahlberg.

Stories For Five-Year-Olds by S.Corrin.

Squirrel Wife by Philippa Pearce.

A Gift From Winklesea by H.Cresswell.

They Came From Aargh by R.Hoban.

Ready-Set-Robot by L. and P. Hoban.

Post-Office Cat by G.E.Haley.

Grump and the Hairy Mammoth by Derek Sampson.

Greyfriars Bobby by Lavinia Derwent.

Animal Ark Series by Lucy Daniels.

For Older Readers

Paddy on the Island by Ursula Moray Williams.

Farthest Away Mountain by L.R.Banks.

Tom's Midnight Garden by P.Pearce.

Wings by T.Pratchett.

Mouse Butcher by D.King-Smith.

Donkey Skin by Perrault.

Chapter 10: <u>WITCHES, GHOSTS & THE OCCULT</u>

"… Live as children of light …"   (Ephesians 5: 8, 12)

F) Is there a harmful pre-occupation with occult themes?

If there has been any *one* cause for concern amongst parents in recent years with regard to children's books, it has surely been the emergence of occult themes growing out of all proportion like a cuckoo in the nest. Significantly, it has also been the area of greatest controversy, since many have argued that there is no difference between witches and fairies, ghosts and goblins: "Why this paranoia? It's only make-believe, isn't it?" The very fact that this issue arouses such contention should alert us to the truth that this is part of that age-old battle, the Cosmic Confrontation referred to in chapter 3.

At the heart of the matter is the difference between the real and the unreal. If we believe that God is the supernatural power for good, we cannot ignore Satan, the source of evil power who, though limited by God, has mastered the art of counterfeit (see Exodus 7:10-12; Acts 13:6, 10). Today, when many are ignorant of Godly principles, the spiritual vacuum is being filled by a phenomenal interest in the occult: that which is *hidden from the natural eye; secret; where there is no light.* Such activity involves a seeking after power and knowledge and *appears* to offer the excitement of the extra-ordinary as an alternative for the perceived restrictions of Christianity. This is of course a deception, since Jesus came to bring freedom and abundant life. (John 10:10). There are some very clear warnings in the Bible against dabbling in occult activity:

"Let no-one be found among you who sacrifices his son or daughter in the fire, who practises divination or sorcery, interprets omens, engages in witchcraft, or casts spells, or who is a medium or spiritist or who consults the dead. Anyone who does these things is detestable to the Lord…" (Deut.18:10-12)

See also Isaiah 47: 8-13; Leviticus 19:31; 20:6 & 27; 2 Kings 17: 16-20;   2Chron.33:6; Rev. 22:15.

If these things were pure fantasy, would God have bothered to prohibit them? The fact that he *has* warned us against them is enough of a deterrent for those who know that he is concerned only for our well-being. The supernatural realm *is* real and can be dangerous. We need to ensure that our children know on whose side they should belong. "Unfortunately, if one discards both God and the devil and then discovers the enchanting world of the supernatural, it is not always the golden champion, King Arthur or Aslan who finds you first, sometimes it is the White Witch" (quoting Lucy Care's article Fairy Stories and the Occult).

There is much evidence of the effects of occultism and sadly it is often the young, being intensely curious, who are caught up in its snare. Dr. Chris Andrew, psychiatrist, has said: "Involvement with the occult can lead to anything from depression and broken relationships to sexual deviation and murder".

Occultism, which has its roots in paganism, surfaces today in many forms. On children's library shelves and in bookshops, it is difficult to avoid titles featuring spirits, psychics, witches, magicians and their mysterious powers. These are addressed here in a separate chapter of their own because they are not about fantasy. Real people are engaged in spiritism and witchcraft. They are bent on recruiting youngsters into their circles and will lead them into situations which are spiritually, mentally and physically harmful.

When assessing books in this category, it is useful first to ask general questions regarding the Cosmic Battle, Horror and Fantasy. Next we must discern whether they are revealing truth, or conditioning the reader to believe falsehood. In *Pangur Ban*, it is more important to save Niall from being bewitched than Finglass from death. The underlying truth is that witchcraft leads to spiritual death, whereas physical death is a door to everlasting life. As we continue to look at examples, we must also consider where is the source of power.

F1.0) Does the story stimulate a child's interest by concentrating on the occult for its own sake?

The cover of *The Farthest Shore* (one of the *Earthsea Trilogy* by Le Guin) announces that "Sparrowhawk undertakes a sea odyssey in search of the source of evil". His quest is for mysterious power for its own sake. This is quite a different matter from finding oneself in the presence of evil and needing courage to resist it (James 4:7).

Several books suggest that it is necessary to unlock the door into another world. *The Key to the Other* gives Flip a "thrill of power" over other people, and though the text gives some warnings against meddling, the story still rouses the readers' excitement. Nick advises that a complete understanding of secret knowledge is better than a little.

The Lost Key (R.Hunt. Oxford Reading Tree: stage 7) tells of a small boy with a problem. "Kipper wanted a magic adventure but the magic key would not glow". Even his family is disappointed. Finally, he takes it to bed with his cuddly toys. The last line reassures us: "Suddenly the magic key began to glow".

The same symbolism is to be found in *Moondial*, where Mr. World the caretaker tells Minty that she is the one to turn the key and help those poor children "on the other side". Minty, who has had ghostly experiences since the age of three and has been contacted by her dead father, deliberately looks for mysterious phenomena. She encounters a pocket of coldness near the moondial and determines to return on her own.

Minty avoids talking to her Aunt Mary, the church-warden, about her suspicions. She "had learned long ago to keep her secrets to herself". Deceit is woven into the story. The word "secrets" is used as a euphemism to mean "hidden (occult) things". "A secret, any secret, was a source of power. She did not put this idea into words; it was simply an instinct she had".

Minty creeps out to the church-yard at midnight. She regards the moondial as a focus of power, a doorway to another time, where she becomes a benign ghost to the children of a previous era. Mr World, who encourages Minty in her pursuits, is the only character who is friendly and helpful. Further deception suggests that children wanting to engage in these intriguing pastimes must actively use their will, but can give them up whenever they choose.

This is just not true. Dr. David Enoch, Fellow of the Royal College of Psychiatrists and one-time consultant to the Royal Liverpool Hospital, warned that those opening their minds to the occult are "unleashing forces into their lives they don't understand and often can't combat" (Church of England Newspaper, 14.10.88).

Dr. Stuart Checkley, psychiatrist, emeritus professor of London University has said: "I have seen patients whose involvement with relatively minor forms of the occult have caused them to suffer mental illness … The symptoms of occult involvement are similar to those of schizophrenia … The occult has a harmful effect through unknown mechanisms". He has seen people who, following lengthy and unproductive psychiatric treatment, will recover after being helped by the church.

Rachel Storm once reported on the case of Ian Thain for The Independent Newspaper. Having an interest in astrology at the age of seven, he was attracted to the power available through occult activity. Giving his testimony, he says –

"You have a secret power over people without them knowing. You think you are in control, whereas really you are a victim. You are on an intravenous drip of evil … I could influence events, make things happen … There is nothing wishy-washy about it. I am an engineer, very practical, I got results".

Now and again he was terrified. At the age of 23, Ian read the passage in Deuteronomy 18 which changed his life. He became a Christian and found release.

Books such as those described in this chapter increase curiosity and provide role-models for children to copy. They promote paranormal practices as exciting and harmless. Light-hearted beginnings, like horoscopes, ouija, tarot and games of levitation, lead on to more thrills, in the same way that drug addicts begin with cannabis, until the whole matter becomes out of control. We are not talking about a handful of isolated cases. In 2011 a survey revealed that in Lancashire schools alone 87% of children had dabbled in the occult, 44% with ouija boards.

The public at large, in dismissing the rather quaint image of the devil with a forked tail, have underestimated the power of evil itself. Any activity deliberately pursued against God's wishes opens the door to Satan's influence in our lives. This is especially so in the case of occultism which opens direct lines of communication to the spirit world.

1.1) Is the reader encouraged to have an unhealthy interest in spirits of the dead?

In spite of these facts there is a worrying quantity of children's fiction which features spirits or ghosts to some degree. There seems also to be much confusion, so let us remember some Biblical truths. The created order of spirit beings are either angels or demons. Both are able to manifest themselves in bodily form and have the power to speak. When people die they do not become either of these. The human spirit lives on but is not free to roam the world, as illustrated by Jesus' parable of Dives and Lazarus (Luke 16:19ff.).

In Ruth Manning Sanders' *Book of Ghosts and Goblins*, the ghosts come back to earth because of a troubled conscience seeking human aid to right a wrong. This is *not* the Christian gospel; we have one life in which to turn to Christ who makes us right with God.

When a concerned mother complained to her local county library about *The Haunting of Cassie Palmer* (by Vivien Alcock), which explains in detail how to conduct a séance and raise spirits, she was told that this is merely the story of "a young girl and her fantasy friend who helps her to come to terms with reality". In fact, the only reality she faces is that of the spirit world. Cassie is the daughter of a medium, "a humble passer-on of messages", who is proud of her clairvoyant powers. She expounds the need for proper training in order to rise to the heights of her career.

Regarding the "fantasy friend", Cassie first encounters Deverill when she calls up his spirit in the graveyard one night. He makes repeated but unexpected appearances. On his behalf, Cassie returns to the cemetery as if compelled and chants an incantation to the friendly spirits: "O come to me! I am ready! I am waiting!" She calls them to help her break the ring of angry spirits clamouring for Deverill to be burnt as a warlock. He escapes to the peace of the grave, thus appearing to justify her efforts.

Mrs. Palmer praises her daughter for her "fine achievement". She says, "You need never be ashamed of the way you used your gift. You used it well". Later she reflects, "Your gift, it came too sudden and too strong. It does sometimes at adolescence and when it does it burns itself out". This is a dangerous message. It implies that teenagers may use up their psychic gifts totally while young and not be bothered by them again. "Just once!" readers may tell themselves, unaware of the difficulty of withdrawing. There *is* a warning in this novel about involvement with unwelcome spirits, but it could be perceived as a challenge, daring readers to prove themselves, to boast, "I'm not scared!"

There is no warning however of the deception. It is implied that anything that is real is worth investigating. The general impression is one of confusion. Who was Deverill? A ghost or a devil, alive or dead? Tom is enticed to drive a stake through his heart, to kill him! Can you kill a dead spirit? The cover portrays him as a handsome hero! Cassie asks, "Why is everything so mixed up, so many questions without answers …?"

Mrs. Palmer explains that in the Dark Ages spiritism was "all mixed up with silly superstition and black magic", implying that now it is more enlightened. A similar message is given in *Shadow Guests* which refers to phenomena which would once have been called magic but are now known to be associated with radiation and vibrations and far more respectable.

The Witch's daughter by Nina Bawden refers to psychic powers as a special gift, whilst in *Black Nest*, Rachel Dixon, suggests that the heroine's Gift is to be sought after. Rosa argues with her brother, "But it's not a *bad* thing, Tom. You know I'd only use it for good". Tom warns, "You don't know what it might do to you. It got to work on your mind before you'd even heard of it. Remember the nightmares. They weren't good". Tom is upset because Rosa is not herself any more. As the climax of the story, Rosa decides not to keep the Gift; she flings her special amber stone into the sea.

She has made the right decision, but how does the reader react? Are we pleased she threw away her Gift? No. Ironically, we are left bewildered and disappointed; we would know more of this power. After all, it seemed harmless enough, having given Rosa useful insight and an uncanny way with animals. If anything, it was like a born-again experience of heightened awareness and an appreciation of creation. "Everything in the garden was vivid, colours brighter, scents stronger, sounds clearer". Only the dangers of using the Gift for selfish ends are emphasised.

This author is not saying there is anything wrong with occult power, only that in the *wrong hands* it can be used dangerously. Even if the reader agrees with Rosa's decision, he will still be led to believe in the fortune-teller and ghosts who are portrayed here as knowledgeable and helpful! How will a child interpret these confused messages? No clear guidance is given. Aunt Hetty tells her to make up her own mind!

F2.0) Is the reader led to empathise, or collaborate with those involved in the occult?

"Do not give the devil a foothold".   (Eph. 4:27)

The aim of a skilful writer is to create a hero so exciting and alive that every young reader will want to identify with him, and even "live out" his adventures in that "safe" fictional realm. If the hero is a *child*, then how much easier to empathise with his motivation and behaviour. How exciting to imitate *Matilda*'s ability to channel power through her eyes! What children do not realise is that channelling is a form of divination, directed by supernatural power, though not from God.

Tim's faithful cat Tobias is in fact a spirit-guide, who first materialises as an astral projection in *Book A1* after Tim has been staring at a picture of a cat. It brings instructions to visit the witch's cottage, with a warning of trouble if he refuses. Tim finds he has no choice: he is being controlled by powers beyond himself, which is of course characteristic of the demonic.

Julia, heroine of *Voices*, having opened the door to dark powers by her interest in the occult, becomes possessed by the alien spirit of old Joshua. By offering his blood in a saucer of warm ashes he had sold his soul to the devil in order to gain learning and power. The spirit of her father also speaks through her. Whilst the reader is immersed in eerie anecdotes, Julia actually loses everything – her father, step-mother, friend, the house. Even her precious silk aeroplane, given her in love, flies away. There has been no plot, neither is she set free from possession. The last line of the book reflects the negative hopeless atmosphere: "Birds only sing when they are angry or frightened". On a 2015 website dedicated to Joan Aiken's work, she is described as one of the U.K.'s most beloved children's authors!

The Bible says that anyone turning to mediums or seeking out spiritists will be defiled by them (Lev. 19:31). It could be argued that children reading this type of book are not personally *using* divination or contacting spirits. But they *are* being encouraged to turn to these dangerous things. They are also being taught how to practise these arts. Likewise, the mind power and E.S.P. previously referred to in chapter 4 are merely modern euphemisms for "occult power".

Whilst teaching children not to be frightened of ghosts, such books condition youngsters to have a favourable, even friendly attitude to them. In *Mr Majeika and the Dinner Lady,* the school governor, who belongs to the Society for Psychical Investigation, is delighted when she finds a ghost in the school. Diana Wynne Jones's *Wild Robert* is another friendly ghost who is really "a nice person underneath". He appears when the heroine summons him from his tomb.

Pamela Oldfield, a one-time infants' school teacher, wrote a collection of *Ghost Stories.* In one, the hero has set up a communication system with a poltergeist. "If I promise to play chess and hold conversations with you and read books to you – will you promise not to do anything too awful?" bargains Gary, who thinks it all great fun but has sworn his sister to secrecy.

Harry Gilbert's *The Ghost's Playground* jumps on all the latest bandwagons. Readers empathise with the ghost who is a young girl, while the heroine, Marion, is Nigerian, with followers-on Faye and Scott, of whom the former is more dominant. Marion boasts that she knows how to deal with ghosts and volunteers to be a spirit-talker. "You have to listen to ghosts, you have to give them what they want, or else!" The ghost dares the children to meet it in the middle of the night in an old air-raid shelter. They enter knowingly into danger and are trapped, but succeed in laying the ghost to rest – "the decent thing to do" – which seems to justify their actions.

2.1) Is the reader led to empathise with witches and wizards or admire their power?

Because wizards and witches, or warlocks as their male counterparts are sometimes known, have been associated with tall hats and broomsticks, or even been confused with fairies, as in Aiken's *The Cat Sat on the Mat*, people have assumed that they are purely fantasy characters. However, these trappings are merely a disguise, a deception which takes our eyes away from real people who actually meet in covens, practise witchcraft and exert a certain amount of power. Their terminology may be different; they may refer to familiars rather than spirit-guides; they may speak of magic rather than clairvoyance, but their power source is basically the same as that of psychics and mediums. The Bible warns:

"A man or woman that hath a familiar spirit, or that is a wizard, shall surely be put to death".   (Leviticus 20:27. King James Bible).

In Ann Lawrence's version of *Merlin*, the most famous of all wizards, the pictorial decoration is clearly occult, showing pentagrams, hexagrams, snakes and yin-yang signs. The book begins with the story of Merlin's mother made pregnant in a convent by a spirit who is part man (of giant stock: Genesis 6:4?). Both he and Merlin wear the Tau cross, a pagan symbol of life originating from the Babylonian god Tammuz. Even so, the wizard is attributed with the gift of prophecy and is said to be so wise that even the archbishops consult him.

To add to the confusion, some authors portray rivalry between supposedly good wizards and evil witches. In *Moon of Gomrath*, Albanac refers to witch magic as worse than that of a wizard. In *Community Magic* (by Patricia Cleveland-Peck), two ordinary children are apprenticed to Wizard Entwhistle who warns it is important to use magic for good. Though he calls himself a "friendly wizard", he is not above threatening to destroy Miss O'Neath, "an evil mage", and terrifying her with bees which wriggle down her neck! Many stories persuade readers that there are two kinds of witch, the bad and the good, the black and the white. Typical is *Cousin Blodwyn's Visit* by A. Vesey, which was a runner-up for the Mother Goose Award, also *Spell Me a Witch* by B. Willard and *To Trick a Witch* by M.Elliot.

Geronomy, the besom broom in *A Wind from Nowhere*, has escaped from the clutches of an evil witch. He warns the blond and blue-eyed Tamsin, "If you mess about with magic you should know what to expect. Them that goes it blind is… in real bad danger". What sounds like good advice, actually insinuates that the more you know of the occult, the safer you are. Geronomy persuades Tamsin to accept his own magical help. He seductively urges Tamsin to ride him: "Come on love … you know you'll enjoy it", but appeals to her to keep it a secret from her mother. Enjoyment seems to be the main criterion. In saving the heroine from a coven of witches complete with demons and familiars, Geronomy loses his own witchiness, implying great sacrifice.

In *Winter Players*, Oaive with her auramantic voice summons a "sort of psychic cloak" which "made her feel invincible". We are given to understand that this witch is not evil − mysterious, yes, rather romantic and close to the natural world, yet saddened by those who do not accept her. How relieved the reader feels when she escapes the dogs which would tear her to pieces.

Inevitably the reader empathises with the good witch, who in fact is calling on the same power as the evil witch using black magic. This empathy is especially keen if the witch or wizard is the main character of the story. Of course, young readers are most likely to identify with witches who are portrayed as children, thus saying, "You can be like me!" Examples include *Titchy Witch* by Jean Bayliss, (which is listed on the Montessori House of Children "Books for Students") and Bessie's grand-children in *To Trick a Witch* who are proficient in spells and E.S.P.

Witchcraft is a family affair in Margaret Mahy's *The Haunting* in which supernatural events are said to "strengthen individual identities and relationships"! When Great Uncle Cole accuses the family of destroying Barnaby's gift, his sister is quick to defend them: "We wouldn't destroy his gift. If he were magic we'd all say, "Go on, be a magician, don't let us stand in your way", and we'd get books out of the library to help him …" The grandparents encourage Troy, "Be a magician with my blessing, my dear". Only great-grandmother renounces magic as wicked, but she is portrayed as "the enemy".

In Uncle Cole we see the lust for power and control: "I'm going to remake the world so that we can live in it and never be seen. I can do that you know and more!" Finally, it is Troy who emerges as the gifted one. She begins by practising astral projection − "casting dreams of the solar system into the darkness she had magicked up in the … sitting room". Sadly, witchcraft *is* practised in families, resulting in abuse of children unable to escape.

Evidence has been brought to light from those who have been rescued out of occult activity that children are prime targets for recruitment into covens. Not only do witches believe that a child's fear lends more power to their ritual, but also that a child at puberty provides the strongest input into a coven's strength. Their presence gives vent to a satanic hatred of childhood stemming from the spirit of Molech, god of child-sacrifice (Jer.32:35). (Compare Chapter 4: 7.4, on pagan gods and goddesses.) In the time of Daniel and his friends Shadrach, Meshach and Abednego, the Babylonian culture of Nebuchadnezzar was intent on stealing away young people from the one true God. The same spiritual forces are at work today.

According to Dianne Core of Childwatch, covens also attract paedophiles because of their reputation for ritual sexual abuse of children. She has been reported as saying,

"Innocence has been taken and destroyed. If the public knew as much as we do or had seen the after effects of the abuse on these young children, I don't think they would ever express doubt again".

Reformed and healed witches testify to the very real power of Satan which only submits to the power of Jesus Christ. Why is all this allowed to happen? It is because widespread disbelief in witchcraft led to the repeal of the Witchcraft Laws in 1952, thus legalising the continuation of such practices.

In another instance reported in the national press, a self-styled "wizard" from Hertfordshire abused thirteen young girls aged between six and early teens. He persuaded them that sex would make them into witches with special powers. How could such children be tricked in this way? It is because they have been conditioned through their story books to accept wizards as friendly and truthful, and witches as helpful to the community.

Maureen Davies, formerly of the Reachout Trust which helps people to recover from the effects of occult involvement, has said that "teachers have a lot to answer for in encouraging children to write essays about witchcraft". Of course, this written work will often have been stimulated by the reading of a story on the same subject.

With the help of a series of short questions, let us look at further examples which give false impressions regarding witches.

2.11) Is the witch portrayed as harmless, even friendly?

At one time, witches were so nasty that no child would want to encounter one, let alone follow their practices. Now, they are "misunderstood", and even *The Worst Witch* (by Jill Murphy) is not so bad. Maybe Old Meg, of *Hey Robin, is* ugly and dirty but she is "a wise woman" and cures warts with her spells. Branded as a witch, her market-stall is vandalised and a dunking in the river threatened. Meg's plight invites our sympathies. The reader cheers Robin as he helps her escape the menacing crowd.

There are many stories which tell of children visiting witches' and wizards' homes and making friends with them. This is a common theme in the reading schemes of Sheila McCullagh. Her *One, Two, Three and Away* series features a poor little witch who needs Benjamin's help. In her Ladybird Reading Programme, *Puddle Lane*, children associate freely with a wizard, right through all five stages, whilst in the *Tim and Tobias* scheme, it is implied that the more Tim is acquainted with Melinda, the "safe witch", the friendlier and more trustworthy she becomes.

Readers of *The Witch V.I.P.* are told: "The witch is the best friend Simon ever had, but there's only one thing Simon can be sure of when she's around – there'll be trouble". Actually the close relationship is rather odd since she scares other children and can even be aggressive towards Simon. The implication is that youngsters should feel sorry for strange women who are regarded with suspicion by the majority. This too is dangerous encouragement to the young and vulnerable, though one would also deplore a certain trend to link witchcraft with lonely old ladies!

2.12) Is there an emphasis on the normality of witchcraft?

Closer to the truth than many would like to imagine are the tales about witches being ordinary people, living in council flats, eating whippy ice-creams in the park, like Pat Kremer's *Tilly Witch*. *The Haunting* conveys a very relaxed attitude. Mahy refers in the same breath to Clair's ability to "call a doctor or find an expert on black magic in the telephone book". It is implied that *Winnie the Witch* (by K.Paul and V.Thomas) becomes normal and well adjusted when she redecorates her black house with bright cheerful colours. However, there is no evidence of her changing her ways.

Witches may indeed be ordinary people, but to describe witchcraft as normal implies acceptability of its practices. Children need to be taught to keep a respectful distance from such activity, for youngsters who do break free from its clutches require counselling, or occasionally rehabilitation. We must not allow children to believe that witches are simply following an alternative but equally valid lifestyle. In striving for a tolerant society, we are mistakenly allowing freedom of expression to enslave its own victims.

2.13) Are witches portrayed as respected members of society?

Many works of fiction are teaching a different kind of respect for witches and wizards, in accord with a revered status in society. In *The Key to the Other*, the Westons claim to be descended from the Magi and the Crusaders and are the librarians of the magic world, owning a priceless collection of occult books. They are an important family in the town. Grandma "does a lot for local charities".

The Times Educational Supplement, reviewing *The Wizard of Earthsea*, has stated: "It is doubtful whether a more convincing and comprehensive account of a sorcerer's training exists anywhere in fiction outside the Earthsea's chapters." Should we then view it as a valuable manual?

J.K.Rowling's *Harry Potter* books promote the idea that witchcraft is respectable, even entertaining. The witchcraft school is an acceptable alternative to Eton! Hidden under a cloak of morality, being polite, honest, considerate and ensuring that good wins over evil, is the overwhelming theme, that of normality and respectability.

Ged is portrayed as a village benefactor, casting spells of increase on the flocks, spells of blessing on tools and looms and protection over houses. The whole ethos of this novel promotes the respectability of sorcery, emphasised by such terms as "craft" and "journeyman wizard". The fact that the inhabitants of Lastland have no witch or sorcerer is intended to illustrate how uncivilised and unenlightened they are.

Community Magic makes the study of the occult sound like joining the Boy Scouts. "In part 2 of the course he (William) could choose his favourite sort of magic". As Community Wizard, Entwhistle receives "a small payment from the Department of Social Sorcery". In a large-print book for 7-8 year-olds, this could be criticised as an adult joke, but more harmful is the insidious message which this and many other books carry promoting the benefit of magic to society.

2.14) Are witches portrayed as helpful people, perhaps healers?

Entwhistle's protégées try very hard "to bring happiness and magic to the people of their village wherever possible". Whilst William has power over animals, his sister is learning to control the weather. The amazing accomplishments of *Tilly Witch* are said to include finding lost items, restoring lost youth, bringing happiness and camaraderie to the people in the park, enabling a boy to catch a golden fish, and curing headaches.

Whilst Blacker's *Ms Wiz* shines as the kindest doctor in the hospital, at hand wherever magic is needed, Tomie de Paola tells us that Granny Witch, owner of *The Magic Pasta Pot*, had such a magic touch that even the nuns and priests visited her with their troubles and were cured of headaches and warts. These messages suggest that magic is completely compatible with Christian beliefs and is even the original healing power.

Authoress Philippa Pearce once reviewed *The Winter Players* in The Guardian with this revealing snippet: "What makes this book remarkable is the from-the-inside sense of the so-called supernatural and of its relevance to human welfare". Christians believe it is the healing that comes in the name of Jesus which is beneficial, not that from counterfeit power.

2.15) Are witches given an attractive, exciting image?

Words such as wonderful, brilliant and special are used to describe *Naughty Natalie's* witchy saviour who is dressed "all in silver with a pointed silver hat and long red hair". At Miss Cackle's Academy for Witches (*The Worst Witch*) the girls admire their teacher Miss Hardbroom with her hair streaming out behind her, looking "splendid in her full witch's robes and hat".

Young people are naturally drawn to whatever seems exciting and fun. *Mr. Majeika,* a wonderful wizard full of surprises, gives the impression that being a magician is an easy life: you make spells and enjoy yourself! Wouldn't every child want a teacher like this one. Simon is certainly excited that the *Witch V.I.P.* is to become his new head-mistress, even if she is a walking disaster.

The very format of Helen Nichols' *Meg and Mog* books is tremendously attractive to infants. Their brightly coloured pages are alive with amusing images. Large clear print, use of speech balloons and novelty lettering grab one's attention (e.g. *Mog's Mumps*). What a pity this is all for the sake of a friendly, fun-loving witch who uses spells to solve her problems!

Of course, the power of a magician is attractive in itself. *The Wizard of Earthsea* had learned as a boy to summon the "fathomless energies of the universe". He longs to attain the height of The Summoner's art − the raising of spirits of the dead − so that he need not fear anything in the world. He is portrayed both as an amazing conjuror and a knowledgeable man of truth.

Modern witchcraft, or Wicca as it is often called, is a meld of eastern and western magic. It traces its origins back to the fertility cults of Babylonian times, to Molech and his female counterpart Ashtoreth, also referred to as Semiramis, Astarte, Ishtar, Isis, the moon goddess, and in Jeremiah 44:25 Queen of Heaven. They were said to rule all the spirits of the dead. Witchcraft, like Satanism, spiritism and spiritualism involves worship of a deity and the use of supernatural power, so all are therefore types of religion.

Nowadays, occultists advertise their practices quite openly on the web. It is not surprising therefore that they are breaking into the world of children's publishing in order to promote the thrills and intrigues, but not the dangers, of their lifestyle.

F3.0) What kind of magic do we find in junior fiction?

3.1) Are there explicit descriptions of occult paraphernalia, encouraging a child to experiment?

The magic that we are concerned with in this chapter is not the enchantment of fantasy, the unexplained element of life which children wonder about. Neither is it the mysterious help from on high when the hero is striving for good to prevail. Rather, it is a sinister power being introduced for its own sake into the imagination of young minds. It appears in various forms, from the scientific to the purely fanciful wish-fulfilment of *Barney Bipple's Magic Dandelions* (Chapman and Kellogg) in which the children wish for material goods toys, food, a pony, a radio: all are granted. This is not the magic which responds to, "If only I could be… or do…", but "If only I could have…"

Magic is described attractively. As *Charlie Dragon* creates a fancy-dress outfit for George, "a glowing golden rush of magic" creeps over him comfortingly, making him "curiously warm". A different kind of attraction draws Tamsin to the magic fungus in *A Wind from Nowhere* − a fascination with its strange beauty.

A Swiftly Tilting Planet is manifestly a work of science fiction, but introduces scrying pools, crystal balls and runes. It refers to seers whose visionary gift comes from the gods, and also from God which is rather confusing! In *The Key to the Other* the author makes the distinction between the "harmless" frippery of Mr. Sparrow's joke-shop, with its magic symbols, and the High Magic of the Westons. She also suggests that the shop is protected from magic but omits to say by what means!

One might expect fantasy and witchy-type titles to feature some occult paraphernalia. Palmistry and astrology are mentioned in *Dragon Paths*. In *Which Witch?* by E.Ibbotson, we find the use of a hollow skull and a magic triangle to invoke the shades of the underworld. Even so, it is a surprise to find details of scrying in young fiction, with water and finger-nails in *Community Magic*, and even in the early reading series *Puddle Lane.*

More disturbing though are such inclusions when no warning is given by outward appearances, as in the case of *Here Comes Charlie Moon*, where chapel-goer Aunt Jean reads tea leaves and a crystal ball. *Sea Baby* (from *More Tales of Shellover*) is a bit of nonsense by Ruth Ainsworth in which a fisherman catches a baby out of the sea. Help from a Wise Woman who consults her crystal is taken for granted. What a pity horoscopes are given credence in Kathleen Gooding's *The Rainbow Trail*, an otherwise excellent story.

Elidor was described by the critics as a beautiful work of poetic imagination and won rave reviews at the time of publication from the Times Ed., The Teacher and The Listener. In this book the planchette, the original ouija board, is enjoyed as acceptable evening entertainment by children and parents alike. Similarly, *Charlotte Sometimes* describes in detail a séance that achieves results. *Voices* not only mentions scrying but also explains *how* to tell fortunes with cards and how to dowse for water.

More unusual is the kind of magic described in Ann Ruffell's *Pyramid Power*. Martin the hero swears compulsively and has a defiant attitude towards his single mum. He learns to tap in to the concentrated energy of a pyramid with healing powers. He is driven on by the promise of knowledge and understanding into transcendental experiences. At a point strategically near the climax, Martin holds back through fear, but by now the reader is willing him on to know more, to go deeper, to open the door to more thrilling adventures.

His Grandpa describes ley-lines as "lines of power". He implies that Christians built churches over them for this reason, having determined their position by dowsing. Jill knows what that means and accuses her ignorant brother of not reading the right books! He eventually discovers an immense power: "all the forces of the earth which he had called up with his pyramid over the crossing ley-lines".

All these practices are methods of divination, i.e. the search for supernatural knowledge which leads to power. Oaive, of *The Winter Players*, is paid to read fortunes. We are told, "She read truly… it is not unpleasant to anticipate good. It hurts no one". Contrast this with Acts 16 where St.Paul was troubled by a slave girl who could predict the future. She proclaimed the truth of the apostles' message, yet Paul discerned the origin of this spirit and cast it out in the name of Jesus.

Books in this genre encourage a latent fascination for the paranormal and increase the urge to experiment, even in the junior age-group. Having been so conditioned through fiction to this "harmless fun", youngsters invited to participate for real will receive no warning signals; the dangers have been diluted.

3.2) Is there explicit information about spells, charms and ritual?

Though *Heggerty Haggerty's* (by E.Lindsey) ghastly brew of toadstools, dandelions and toasted slime may seem like fun, when words of spells are printed in the text one should be wary. The power of the word is very real. Garner advises that the spells he uses for *Moon of Gomrath* are authentic (though incomplete, just in case) and are taken from magical manuscripts in the British Museum and Bodleian Library.

The *Dungeons and Dragons Rule Book* instructs readers to memorise each spell, often from actual books of magic, speak it aloud and reabsorb it in order to use it again. In *A Wind from Nowhere* one reads spells in the text, whilst in *A Necklace of Raindrops,* Aiken writes of the benefits of wearing an amulet. In the Holmes McDougall third *Resource Reader*, amongst excellent extracts from E.B.White's *Charlotte's Web* and Ingalls Wilder's *Little House on the Prairie,* we find a chapter describing Abracadabra as an Assyrian god. As an exercise, readers are encouraged to trace this magic word many times over for an amulet!

Counterfeits of Christian exorcism are evident when spells are used in *Odin's Monster* to release imprisoned spirits and lay them to rest, or as binding influences by Ged and Oaive. In *The Great Ghost Rescue*, Eva Ibbotson insinuates that clergymen use rowan berries and pentacles in their ghost-laying spells! Charms and spells often involve the use of ritual. Whilst Cassie Palmer learns how to make a wax voodoo doll, *The Ghost of Thomas Kempe* is eventually caught by summoning him with a cleft rowan stick into a circle of ancient symbols.

Belladonna, a major character in *Spell Me a Witch*, is given the status of Necromancer. When a baby is left on her doorstep she views it with distaste but resists the urge to throw it away, supposing it may come in useful for advanced spells! She teaches her students to be nasty and malicious, swears by Lucifer and Hades and utters incantations in both English and Latin. In attempting to free Angelica from an embarrassing enchantment, a knife, wand, pentacle, amulet, sword and yew slivers are all employed, but it is the baby's tears collected in a crystal flask which prove to be the only solution. Recognise here the spirit of Molech!

In the *Tim and Tobias* series we can trace the development of a theme. Book B8 at the second level contains a picture of a witches' coven around a fire encircled by trees. At level three, the introduction of Grandmother Roon with her bright blue eyes brings the subject closer to home. She reappears in Book D3 as the instigator of a ceremony held at a flat altar-like stone. With incantation and the power of the moon as essential elements, she presents Tim with a shield-stone carved with strange signs for his protection.

The *Humming Bird* series by the same author includes the title *Hallowe'en*, in which a coven is depicted dancing over the flames of a Samhain fire, whilst a family is seen enjoying the same festival at home. According to *T.R.Bear's Hallowe'en*, those not in favour of trick or treating are regarded as "stuffed shirts", thus justifying the jamming of their door-bells and daubing of windows. This "very ancient folk ceremony" is regarded as good fun! "Why wait till Samhain to go apple-bobbing, dress up and dance around a black cat chanting spells?" tempts Susan Hill in *Mother's Magic*. Lottie's friend, about six years old, holds such a party on her *birthday*. This book confuses the different kinds of magic and suggests they are all to be welcomed.

In contrast, Dr. Russell Blacker, psychiatrist and member of the Christian Medical Fellowship, has said, "Children should be guarded from the ideas of power, subjugation, death and destruction which are sold at Hallowe'en … they cannot have a good effect on children."

This pagan occasion, with roots in druidism and witchcraft, celebrates and identifies with the powers of darkness and glorifies death. It is sad therefore that Hallowe'en is mentioned in the most unexpected settings with no bearing on the plot.

F4.0) Is the overall treatment of the theme a true and balanced representation of occultism?

4.1) Is the book likely to worry or frighten the reader?

So far this chapter has concentrated on the propaganda which persuades readers that occultism is harmlessly exciting. However, some authors over-emphasise the fear and horror associated with death and the spirit world:

"…a fiery chariot lit up like Hell all reddy and full of demons in dreadful hats all screeching and laughing…."

With passages like this from Dorothy Edwards' *The Witches and the Grinnygog*, it is obvious that a child does not have to indulge in the horror fantasies of Jackson and Livingstone to be frightened by the supernatural. This story and others like it are intended to scare. Spine-chilling details of a Hallowe'en curse come too close for comfort in Keith Lillington's *The Hallowe'en Cat*. Mike hears the howling and scratching of a black cat as its shadow appears on his bedroom window. It stares darkly at him from a tree just outside, and then disappears.

Equally worrying for the very young must be the ghostly picture-books like *The Ghost-Eye Tree*, or Mahy's *The Witch in the Cherry Tree* with witches that appear convincingly real in the garden. A friend told me of her three-year-old's fear of old ladies which she felt must have something to do with story book pictures of witches.

Dahl's *Witches* left an eleven-year-old girl not only frightened but confused. The preface states that this book is not a fairy tale, but is about real witches. Though they look quite ordinary, they are vile and cunning and hate children. Having convinced the reader he is stating fact, the writer digresses into error: "In England there are about one hundred of them … no such thing as a male witch …". Fantasy takes over with the explanation that a ghoul is always male and so is a barghest. Grandmother describes how witches force parents to kill or eat their offspring by turning them into slugs, fleas or even hot-dogs! Having pressed home his warning against witches, Dahl assures us that they have all now been utterly wiped out by their own magic mixture. What is a child to believe?

For those who are frightened, where is the reassurance of protection from equally valid supernatural forces for good? Are they taught how to resist evil with Christian weapons of love, prayer, faith and the power of the Holy Spirit? The problem is as much disinformation as misinformation. In contrast, Jenny Robertson's *Circle of Shadows* tells of a boy in the time of the Roman persecution of Christians who is helped by the persistent love of a friend to overcome the effects of occult Celtic rites.

The Witch of Witchery Wood by Joan Cass is not overtly Christian, yet conveys the right messages without being too scary regarding the danger of secret meetings with witches. All ends happily, though it is clear that the townsfolk begin again to underestimate the witch's power after the crisis has blown over! However, perhaps the author gives too high a profile to Molly Millikins. Hers is a far more developed characterisation than the princess, who is supposedly the heroine but does not enter the story till the second chapter. Unfortunately it is quite probable that readers will find the witch the more interesting of the two!

4.2) Does the book, series or collection stimulate a child's expectancy of occult activity or exploit its entertainment value?

So vast is the number of books available that contain reference to the occult that it is quite possible that any particular collection, be it class bookshelf, the school or public library, or a child's own selection will contain a disproportionately high percentage on this theme. Avid readers will be receiving an unbalanced reading diet, some even becoming obsessed and choosing only these books, as with J. K. Rowling's successful *Harry Potter* series. Being a skilful writer, she is able to draw the reader on to increasingly horrific scenes from one chapter to the next, from one book to the next, pandering to the baser desires for nasty and nastier images. There will be an expectancy for this kind of excitement; other subjects will seem bland in comparison.

Notice the build-up of witch-consciousness throughout certain reading schemes. In the *One, Two, Three and Away* scheme we find at the lower levels the odd witchy or ghosty book tucked in amongst stories of Billy Blue Hat, until at the higher levels and extension readers the vocabulary has been acquired for books that dwell on the mystery of the occult.

In the *Tim and Tobias* series, new elements are added at each level, progressing from one safe witch to the fearsome Wind Witches and the Strange People born of human mothers and ghost fathers! Such is the skill of the author that the climax of every book leaves the reader on a cliff-hanger, compelled to move on to the next until every one of the thirty-two stories has been absorbed. This series has often been used to help late developers and could well comprise their entire diet of school readers for two or three years.

Browsing through *The Prediction Book of the Tarot* (by M.Montalban), which I found in a town library in the section labelled "Books for Young People", I came across the following statements:

"Magic is the study of the natural laws …" One who has studied these is "a priest of the gods … Do not be afraid to use occult power … not evil, simply sensible".

Many of the stories our children read express exactly the same sentiments as this between the lines of an exciting plot. However, whilst demonstrating an alternative source of power, they also present an unbalanced view of the spiritual realm where demons are legion, angels are few and Christianity is irrelevant. God's certain power is not mentioned; his protection is ignored.

Ironically, the effect of this surfeit of evil supernatural is evident in a picture book intended to entertain, entitled *Well I Never* by Heather Eyles. Described as "a perfect and delightful mixture of fear and fun", this is the story of a totally disorganised punky mother and her young daughter whose head is so full of witchy images that she encounters weird spectres in every room of her house. They even follow her to school. These vampires and were-wolves are also worming their way into the minds of the five-year-olds who choose this book and others like it − for fun!

To provide such books for education or entertainment is unhelpful. Biblical truth is being passed over in favour of idolatrous pagan practices. Obviously we would not want to ban all stories with a supernatural theme or a mention of witches. However, responsible adults will want to protect their children's minds and teach them to avoid evil.

If occult power is portrayed as the force for good, what place is left for God? There is a great need to redress the balance by recognising God's almighty power and blessing. Let us return to traditional values, even though relativism may be more politically correct!

Recommended Books

One Moonlight Night   by R. and D. Armitage.

Hagbane's Doom   by J. Houghton.

Farthest Away Mountain   by Lynne Reid Banks.

Narnia Series   by C.S. Lewis.

The Web   by Peggy Burns.

Circle of Shadows   by Jenny Robertson.

Chapter 11: <u>HUMOUR – WHAT ARE CHILDREN LAUGHING AT?</u>

"Nor should there be any obscenity, foolish talk or coarse joking which are out of place…"   (Eph. 5:4)

G) Are our children being taught to laugh inappropriately?

G1.0) Are children being taught to enjoy dark humour?

When it comes to humour we touch on an area which is highly subjective. What causes one individual to rock with laughter might well leave another cold. There are an infinite number of situations which *could* tickle one's sense of fun, ranging from the intellectual play on words to the more outrageous throwing of custard pies. Our reasons for laughing are many and varied: from surprise, embarrassment, incredulity, with derision, to happiness and fun.

Youngsters enjoy being entertained. They have an uncomplicated sense of humour, being easily reduced to giggles! They are not naturally cynical or sarcastic. Teachers choose to read amusing stories to their classes because these are an effective medium through which to drive home serious messages. Any who have chuckled at Paddington Bear (*More About Paddington* by Michael Bond) redecorating his bedroom will at the same time have been alerted to the foolishness of tackling single-handedly tasks beyond their capabilities!

It is not the intention of this investigation to judge whether certain material is amusing, or whether *youngsters* will find it so. The aim is simply to reveal what they are *expected* to enjoy as humour by authors offering their work in this category in order that *you* may decide whether or not you desire your children to laugh at subjects which are not intrinsically funny.

Whilst recognising the current trend for alternative comedy, we would surely prefer our children to use discretion and learn to weigh humour for themselves − to step back and question, "What am I laughing at?" and to reject the humour that urges them to laugh cruelly, disrespectfully, obscenely or sinfully.

However, Christian values are not instinctive; they must be taught. Children left to themselves are in danger of sinking to the lowest common denominator if not checked or inspired otherwise, as William Golding so graphically showed in *Lord of the Flies*. School-boy humour is aptly named. It is the responsibility of parents and teachers to guide their children's innate sense of fun into wholesome outlets. These final sections therefore develop certain questions that we may ask of any books that children read.

1.1) Are children being taught that sin is to be laughed at?

Sometimes it is difficult to tell whether an author is being serious or not. John Prater's *On Friday Something Funny Happened* is a picture-book. Each day of the week two children run riot through a series of situations − home, park, supermarket and so on leaving a trail of disaster behind them. Unlike Paddington, these brats are undisciplined and naughty. Only half a parent is ever seen, let alone heard. The fact that Friday, when the pair are quiet, is reckoned to be funny underlines the point the writer is making: that it is really the other six days that are hilarious. We find ourselves laughing at disorder and chaos.

Often the illustrations indicate whether or not comedy is intended: exaggeration and caricature go hand in hand with humour. So it is obvious that we are expected to smile at Captain Pugwash (*Pugwash and the Sea Monster* by J.Ryan) when he attempts to outwit his rival pirate, Cut-Throat Jake. When Willie sits on a cactus spike, youngsters will chuckle, not with derision because he is a villain, but with delight because he is funny. Are they also expected to laugh with approval when Pugwash sails away with all the stolen treasure for himself?

Should youngsters laugh when values are turned upside down? Mahy's *The Very Wicked Headmistress* uses coarse expressions and sings suggestive cabaret songs. She also cheats the parents and resorts to blackmail. With the style of "007" she attempts a shotgun wedding with a Colt Peacemaker in order to inherit a diamond fortune. A threatening custard mountain saves the day, but she escapes unrepentant to continue her life of crime.

In complete contrast, we giggle with incredulity at little old lavender-scented Miss Amity in *Jeffey the Burglar's Cat* by Ursula Moray Williams. We share the shame and exasperation of Jeffey who deplores her criminal activities but delights in her ultimate decision to turn over a new leaf. With the intervention of the kindly bishop, the reader may infer that a Christian influence has played a part in her transformation!

As hinted in a previous chapter, witches and ghosts provide plenty of scope for ungodly humour. In *Spell Me a Witch*, where the school motto is "Fair is foul and foul is fair", the heroine is wicked and mischievous, while her friend gains top marks in Spiteful Intention. The fact that stories like this and *The Witch V.I.P.*, or even *Gus Was a Gorgeous Ghost* by Jane Thayer, are very funny does not mean they are innocent of deception.

There is certainly plenty of malevolence in *Little Dracula at the Seaside*, that is, underneath all the superficial jokiness. Minutely detailed drawings call for closer inspection, revealing skulls, graves, blood, ghosts and dragons. At the fair, the family meet their witchy friends who tell fortunes by tarot cards, tea leaves and a crystal ball, and "all had lots of fun".

As young readers enjoy the escapades of fictional friends, they become partners with them in the action. It is worth heeding the writer of Proverbs 20:11 who said: "Even a child is known by his actions, by whether his conduct is pure and right".

1.2) Are children being encouraged to laugh at indecency and vulgarity?

To assume that a best selling author is also a great writer would be to draw careless conclusions. The fact that the type of comedy Roald Dahl specialises in attracts young readers does *not* prove its excellence. If it did, then comics would become classics! Given Dahl's macabre sense of humour, it is quite likely that he had the last laugh – at those giving him rave reviews for his vulgarity! He himself once advised writers of young fiction (as quoted in the Times), "to be even more daring and more bizarre. And then go further still". Let us look at the subjects Dahl has used in the name of humour.

He appears to have a pre-occupation with saliva. The reader of *The B.F.G.* is forced to watch the giant sleeping: "Every now and again a big bubble of spit formed between his two open lips and then it would burst with a splash and cover his face with saliva". In *The Witches*, the kitchen-boys spit on the meals they prepare for complaining customers, whilst the story of *Danny* contains a four-line paragraph describing the game-keeper's spit.

Dahl seems to take particular delight in ridiculing women. Notice the use of the feminine gender in this quote from *The Witches*: "It is always funny when you catch someone doing something coarse and she thinks no one is looking. Nose-picking for example or scratching her bottom". He develops this idea when *Matilda*'s cronies put itching-powder in the headmistress's knickers: "She started scratching herself like mad down below… In the middle of the Lord's Prayer she leapt up and grabbed her bottom and rushed out…"

Dahl is not the only children's author by any means to resort to underwear for a cheap laugh. In David Wilson's *What Happened to the Golden Goose*, readers are treated to the spectacle of the king and queen dressed only in their rather modern undies. After the fourth mention of knickers in *The Witch V.I.P.*, one has the firm impression the word is being used quite gratuitously to prop up the giggle factor.

In *The Twits* (R.Dahl), underwear has been dispensed with altogether. When four boys are stuck in a tree, they make their escape by slipping out of their trousers and running for home, "their naked bottoms winking in the sun". Since nudity is always good for a laugh, Linda Allen decides to place *Mrs Simkin's Bath Tub* (level 4 of *Longmans Reading World*) in all manner of public places. Her husband soaks himself on the staircase, in the lounge, on the front lawn --- until all the neighbours follow suit with a bath on their rooftops!

For sure, this fun is cleaner than the toilet type humour. Arabella, at *Dr Monsoon Taggert's Amazing Finishing Academy* (by Andrew Matthews), needs a translation when told that the Dalmatian is "strainin' 'is spuds out in the front yard … You know, gettin' rid o' the water! Dogs, lampposts, d'you get it?"

Anyone not accustomed to discussing bladders and their functions *will* be after encountering *The Sniff Stories* by Ian Whybrow. When it is not Sniff relieving himself in the playground, it's Ben's baby sister wetting her pants. The dog shaking her sodden nappy all over the garden appears to be one of the comic highlights. Though Ben mentions the possibility of suing one's parents for abuse, the *writer* comes very near the mark in his details of little Sal's personal hygiene!

The greatest indignity, verging on the pornographic, is found in Tony Ross's *I Want My Potty*, with its explicit pictures on several pages of a little princess on her pot. She eventually has an accident. Who will laugh at this?

What do we find children laughing at in *Nicobobinus*, a large extravagantly produced volume in fairy tale style by Terry Jones? Rosie drops a chamber pot, spraying its contents all over the corridor. The hero jumps into a "cart-load of high-class excrement" and becomes "a piece of living manure" as he leaps on to the Abbot's lawn, "ordure flying this way and that".

Such images are commonplace in Raymond Briggs' *Fungus the Bogeyman*, set in the unedifying but fitting environment of a sewer. Perhaps the repulsiveness of this book will attract readers? One incensed mother, writing to protest to the School Library Service and to the publisher, suggested incineration might be an appropriate way to eliminate such garbage. She also felt the need to apologise for the kind of words it had been necessary for her to use. She said, "They are very alien to my everyday life – but it only confirms just how unsuitable this book is for children".

Defenders of Briggs' style would argue that he draws on playground language and humour. Of course, children do have a natural interest in bodily functions, but surely this is not to be indulged or exploited for entertainment's sake? Youngsters need to learn both a respect for personal hygiene and an awareness of socially acceptable behaviour. A sensible approach to matters of a private nature is taken in *Body Noises* by Buxbaum and Gelman. One wonders if adults who display an immature obsession with vulgarity are deficient in their own personal development. Dahl for one has admitted, "I have a very childish mind" (quote from a Jonathan Cape publicity poster).

1.3) Are children being taught to laugh disrespectfully?

Super Gran Rules O.K. by Forrest Wilson is just one example of poking fun at those in authority. When she test-drives her futuristic Skimmer illegally and dangerously, she comes face to face with the law. Knowing he has several charges against her, she accelerates away from the flabbergasted policeman. Circling the lake, she drives straight for him, barely clearing his head. What hilarity as he falls into the water. This is no reckless car-thief who will receive his just deserts; this is Super Gran, our heroine, whom children love!

Others standing in the line of fire are head-teachers, vicars and the elderly. Parents too are the target for some barbed humour. Dahl makes the cynical observation on the first page of *Matilda* that proud parents boasting of the achievements of their offspring make one sick. Taking revenge on them by trickery is intended to be amusing. Matilda's "new game" of punishing her parents makes life more bearable.

On passing out of *Dr Monsoon Taggert's Academy*, Arabella feels brave enough to stand up to her parents who have forced her to eat so much that she is teased mercilessly for being fat. "I'm fed up with quips about cub-packs using my knickers as a tent". It is implied that this ten-year-old has been foolish to obey her parents. As she turns the tables, telling *them* they are overweight, readers will smile vengefully.

Large women are always an easy target. When the magic key renders *Tim and Tobias* invisible, in Book A2, they seize the chance to secretly visit the fair, where our hero tests his changed state by pulling a rude face at a fat lady. There is no need for the text to mention her size, except to poke fun.

1.4) Are children learning to laugh cruelly at misfortune?

When *Tatty Apple* steals the chocolates and Mrs Price gives chase, the children run "half-weeping, half-choking with silent laughter" as she stumbles over a dog and comes "rolling down the middle of the steep road … pink petticoat all muddied, big pink legs kicking…" Bound by the secrecy of involvement with magic, the children show no inclination to help the poor woman, to explain or to apologise.

What *is* being offered as humour in the extract from *Skinny Willy* (by W.C.H.Chalk), chosen for inclusion in the 4th *Resource Reader*? From the title we anticipate fun. A lighted banger is dropped into one victim's coat-pocket and into another's letter box. The man who arrives to confront the culprit slips and hits the frying pan handle. "Hot fat went all over his head and down his neck!" Skinner's quip expresses no concern: "Mum and I picked him up off the floor and he was a bit annoyed I think". This makes a joke of a very nasty accident. Similarly, in *The B.F.G.*, both Sophie and the queen are hoping that the butler will fall off his ladder with a crash, silver coffee-pot and all!

Little Nose the Joker is a Neanderthal boy whose practical jokes tend to backfire. Author John Grant wisely points out, "The best jokes are those where everyone laughs, not just the joker". But is this reminder, placed at the end of the book, too far removed from the incidents themselves to be effective? Little Nose himself seems undeterred. He pulls the string that collapses the jackdaw's perch. Is one meant to laugh when the bird falls on its head? Its owner enquires, "Who has been playing tricks?", but Little Nose's motive is purely revenge since Greywing has often pecked him.

When Uncle Redhead reminisces about spreading bear-grease on the floor to make people slip over, mother protests that it wasn't funny, for it was *she* that fell over. Little Nose thinks it hilarious, and it is *his* reaction that readers will remember. Humour directed at another's disaster is callous, but children do not analyse their own behaviour.

Some would protest that the incidents related here are merely of the Tom and Jerry type: surely no one can seriously object to cartoon humour even if it does make fun of the most appalling calamities? I believe there is a clear distinction between that pure fantasy medium, where we know the flattened celluloid Tom will soon bounce back, and the world of literature which becomes real in the imagination.

1.5) Are children being encouraged to laugh at the macabre and the grotesque?

Even more disturbing is that other kind of humour that is sometimes called "the sick joke". It could be defined as that which is actually macabre or grotesque. As discerning adults, we feel a check in our spirit that prevents us from enjoying it.

We need look no further than Alan Ahlberg's *Mrs Jolly's Joke Shop* for a variety of examples. Take a Jolly Joke Card:−

Q. What do you get if you pour boiling water down a rabbit hole?

A. Hot cross bunnies.

The Jollys laugh at everything, even when the window-cleaner's ladder breaks and he comes crashing through the glass. There is no blood, no pain. The incident is presented as fun. Stranger still, at 5 p.m. it begins to rain, by 8 p.m. the town is flooded and at 9 p.m. there is an earthquake! Why are these events brought into the story? It must be a joke! The Jollys sit on their roof splitting their sides laughing. There is no sense of tragedy, no clearing up, no aftermath. It is surely in bad taste to treat so sensitive a subject in such a superficial way. Yet this is one of a series of books claimed by the Children's Rights Workshop as "the greatest thing since Dr. Seuss". According to Google Books, "This title is suitable for reading and sharing at home and at school. It is guided by an Education Adviser, Brian Thompson, and written by an award-winning author"!

In chapter 3 we considered the pagan belief that: Nastiness = Power. Now we find that: Nastiness = Entertainment. In *Little Dracula at the Seaside*, Mrs Dracula fries brains from a severed head for breakfast. *In Stitches with Ms Wiz* includes, with the inevitable bed-pan type jokes associated with hospitals, the horrendous spectacle of the teacher eating Jack's appendix which has crawled out of its bottle on to a plate of red cabbage!

Equally revolting is the fate of the toffee-nosed princess (*The Worm and the Toffee-Nosed Princess,* short stories by Ibbotson).When at last rescued out of the Worm's belly she is covered in bits of mince: "You know what the insides of squashed animals are like… she was wet… crumpled and… bald". Is there any hope for the repentant maiden? "No-one came to marry her… and serve her right". This collection, bridging the gap between picture-books and more substantial works, and presented as humour for young children, concludes with a tale about *The Brollachan.* Here there is very little story, just a description of nastiness. Having been nagged for not being sufficiently vile, the creature eventually eats his mother!

David Wilson's humour also is deliberately macabre. When the King dies, in *What Happened to the Golden Goose*, Dummling holds a party. Mona thinks this is "killingly funny". When *her* head is eventually chopped off, it rolls over the floor giggling, to the loud cheers of the crowd!

In Terry Deary's *The Ghosts of Batwing Castle*, Molly and Wilkin are guided through the Chamber of Terrors. Even though the exhibits are not for child-viewing, they are described to young readers for the sake of black humour. Also for their delight, the resident vampire deals out grisly justice for the obnoxious Wilkin.

Encouraged by his initial success with *Charlie and the Chocolate Factory*, which begged acceptance of the rough justice meted out to those insufferable children, Dahl went on to devise even more gruesome fates for his evil characters. Remember *The Twits,* and the ghastly aunts of *James and the Giant Peach,* "ironed out upon the grass as flat and thin and lifeless as a couple of paper dolls."

Apart from death, all manner of horrific images are presented in a facetious way. The young witches in *Spell Me a Witch* put "tiny curses" on Belladonna: "May her eyes drop out … may her talons curl inwards … may icicles hang from her eyebrows". Of course these are not meant to be taken seriously, but the thought of eyes dropping out is not very funny. A similar flippancy is found in the story of *Nicobobinus* when the doctor prepares to cut off the hero's golden feet. Rosie protests that he will bleed to death. "Well, that's his look out", retorts the doctor.

The intention of both Alice Schertle's *The Gorilla in the Hall* and Chris Riddell's *Mr Underbed* is to poke fun at childish fears of monsters in the dark, but does this treatment really work? These fears may seem absurd in daylight, perhaps surrounded by friends in the classroom, but after dark the images from these picture-books may well return to accentuate the problem and increase the fear.

What should one make of Tomi Ungerer's *The Three Robbers*? Three fierce men dressed in black hold up carriages, smash the wheels with a huge red axe and terrify the victims. One day the robbers encounter a little girl on her way to live with a wicked aunt – why? She is delighted to meet the robbers – why? They bundle her up and carry her away, but she is quite content to live in their cave. She persuades them to spend all their stolen money, to gather up lost or unhappy children and all live together in a castle! The robbers become "kind foster fathers". If this is not funny, what is its purpose? Imagine having to answer a child's questions! Would you be happy for your child to read about youngsters being fostered by evil men?

Even humour is capable of deception; it can cause us to take our eyes off what is right and persuade us that since entertainment is not harming anyone, it must be good, Humanism holds the view that, "Happiness is everything". However the writer of Proverbs 4:20 says:

"My son, pay attention to what I say; listen closely to my words.

Do not let them out of your sight; keep them within your heart;

For they are life to those who find them and health to a man's whole body."

Children need to be protected from a self-centredness that says, "This is funny. I shall laugh because I am enjoying myself. My being happy is all that matters." They need guidance to discern whether certain types of humour are *worthy* of their enjoyment.

G2.0) Are children expected to laugh senselessly?

Some nonsense stories, in traditional fantasy style, clarify reality or underline a deeper truth. Tarbitt's *The Land of Mean-What-You-Say (Tandem Readers Book 2)* causes us to laugh at the strange colloquialisms we use, like "make the bed" or "night *falls*". Donald Bissett's *Upside Down Land* (from *Time and Again Stories*) answers the question, "What if everything were reversed?" So when mice chase cats and the milkman pulls the cart, the reader's subconscious rejects the reversal of normality. However, another of Tarbitt's tales, *Upside-Down Day (Tandem Readers bk.1)*, in which teachers change places with their pupils, is simply an excuse for children to take revenge.

Neither does Aiken's *There's Some Sky in This Pie* bear the hallmarks of true fantasy, but merely calls for inane laughter at its absurdity. A woman bakes a corner of the sky into her apple pie. It is so light that she flies through the sky on it, collecting a pilot, a duck, and a mountain goat as passengers. It finally lands in the sea and becomes an island. What promised to be an "If only" story is disappointingly vacuous.

Maurice Sendak's *In the Night Kitchen*, for 3-6 year-olds, is "another superbly original picture-book", according to the cover blurb. Micky hears a noise in the night. He falls out of bed, out of his pyjamas, through the darkness to the kitchen downstairs where he is mixed into a cake batter by a mysterious chef. He dives into a milk-bottle singing:

"I'm in the milk and the milk's in me.

God bless the milk and God bless me".

As if that were not surreal enough, Micky stands on the bottle's shoulder wearing nothing but a large cup on his head crying, "Cock-a-doodle-doo!" If there is any sense in this it is very obscure. Perhaps its message is that strange, unpredictable events are likely to happen to children when they go to sleep at night! If not, we must assume that this is merely comedy. Does Sendak intend infants to laugh at a chaotic world with no meaning or purpose?

Many of Donald Bissett's stories are completely nonsensical, so much so that it is difficult to summarise them. *Time and Again Stories* left my own sons somewhat baffled. In his *Sleep Tight Snakey Boo*, we find snakes buying ice-creams and a garden taking a holiday! In another of the series, *The Joyous Adventures of Snakey Boo,* we may be able to accept, in the name of fantasy, a ladybird buying a frying-pan, even a steamboat that talks, but when it comes to a microscopic beetle who owns a fridge, that really is stretching the bounds of credibility, especially when Snakey says, "I hope he's making friends with the fridge!"

It has often been said that God has a sense of humour, and certainly there is no reason why God-fearing people should not enjoy comedy:

"There is a time for everything ... a time to weep and a time to laugh" (Ecc.3:4)

On the other hand, to laugh senselessly would seem to lack integrity and make a mockery of true wit.

G3.0) Does the book contain adult humour?

When reading aloud to children one is sometimes aware of a touch of cynicism in an author's work which would be more suitable for adult appreciation. In Bissett's *Joyous Adventures*, he explains that the nature of a prophet is to foretell the future, to "live in the desert and eat locusts and wild honey and wear *lion* cloths… And they cry a lot…" (my italics). Bear in mind that from the level of humour, this book is for the very young! In identifying the snail as a prophet who composes nonsense poetry, the author is making a derisory comment.

Gathorne-Hardy appears to be casting doubts on human sincerity in his tale of *Cyril Bonhamy v. Madame Big*. He implies that characters like Cyril who are paid to dress up as Santa really have no concern for children. Cyril chases his young customers out of the Christmas Grotto brandishing a lead pipe. He runs amok through the toy department, managing to "resist a desire to hurl a horrid boy over the balcony". Children tend to take words at face value. They would not readily discern the sarcasm when the manager exhorts Cyril to, "Get out on those roofs, get down those chimneys. *Be* Father Christmas!"

To adults, the dry humour of Graham Oakley's *Church Mice* series is obvious. Irony is written between the lines of this everyday story of vestry folk. Readers are told, in *A Church Cat Abroad*, that actors "were paid billions of pounds a week plus their bus fares. With that much money …they could not only mend the vestry roof, but buy a patent expanding everlasting cake-frill for the parson".

In *The Church Mice at Christmas*, the vicar is seen watching a dracula-type villain on television, whilst surrounded by cards announcing peace. In a later picture a burglar puts his feet up in a cosy police cell, enjoying Christmas cake and a copy of Playboy! The messages here are certainly above the heads of picture-book readers, as is the quotation: "The best laid schemes o' mice and thingummies gang aft a-gley" *Parents* reading this book will no doubt enjoy the comment on the uselessness of market research, when Humphrey informs them that years of intensive scientific surveys had proved conclusively that parsons don't like crystallised fruits", but what will youngsters make of that?

Obscure adult humour also appears in Mahy's *The Birthday Burglar*, which could otherwise be recommended as a light-hearted piece of frivolity. Simpson is asked,

"Have you got the guilty party tightly?"

"Tight as a lord", he answers.

"That's the wrong sort of tightness," explains Joanna.

The ultimate irony occurs in *Community Magic* when the headmaster is deceived by the evil mage, Miss O'Neeth. He pronounces her books "excellent mainstream fairy tale material". Here is a blatant warning which the author knows will pass unheeded. Who has the last laugh, at the teacher's expense? Isn't this act of derision essentially the same as Tim pulling a face at the fat lady to test his invisibility?!

In closing this chapter I would like to mention just a few titles that would earn full marks from me. Arnold Lobel's *Frog and Toad Together* is a gentle humour which reveals real insight into human nature. Eve Sutton also uses an animal story to give encouragement to timid children. *My Cat Likes to Hide in Boxes* illustrates how life is more exciting if you do not tuck yourself away.

In Derek Sampson's *Grump and the Hairy Mammoth*, the hero assumes the mammoth is to be feared because of his great size. This is no symbolically evil monster. The young reader realises that the creature is only trying to help and protect Grump. In each chapter some calamity results in a new step forward for mankind – the invention of the ladder, fur boots, and so on. Sampson's comical insults are in far better taste than Dahl's. The mammoth is addressed as "cowardly carpet-bag", "barmy beast" and "great furry faggot" (i.e. a meatball!).

In Philippa Pearce's *Lion at School*, a beast comes into the classroom to make a point about cowardly bullies, and also on keeping one's word. This is one of a collection by Sara and Stephen Corrin. The title, *Stories for Five-Year-Olds*, is unfortunate since children of a couple of years above this age-group would appreciate it.

Readers of seven and upwards would enjoy *One Moonlit Night* by R. and D. Armitage, in which two boys laugh at themselves for being scared of camping out in the garden. Even though their sister dresses up as a ghost, it serves to emphasise that there is no such thing in the garden. In fact the boys are brave enough to shout, "Go away and leave us alone!" In the end it is poor dad who gets no sleep!

I suspect that children enjoy humorous stories most of all and, of course, comedy may occur across the whole literary spectrum. For these reasons it is so important for responsible adults to be watchful and discerning over the way humour is exploited, and to teach youngsters to appreciate only the best.

Recommended Books

For Younger Readers

My Friend Mr. Morris by Pat Thompson.

Can You Hear Me Grandad by Pat Thompson.

The Nest by B.Wildsmith.

Hiccup Harry by C.Powling.

For Older Readers

Typically Jennings by A.Buckeridge.

Jeffrey's Joke Machine by A. McCall Smith.

The Incredible Adventures of Professor Branestawm by Norman Hunter.

A Parrot in the House by Linda Allen.

The Gadget War by Betsy Duffey.

Chapter 12: <u>ACTION STATIONS !</u>

"…Therefore, prepare your minds for action…" (1Peter 1:13)

"…making the most of every opportunity…" (Eph. 5:16)

My intention throughout this investigation has been to expose harmful messages in children's fiction, but if I have merely driven readers to despair, then I have laboured in vain. Whilst appreciating the seriousness of the problem, it is important not to be overcome by it, for there *are* good books available which are worth searching out. Rather, my aim has been to stimulate public awareness which will stir up effective action of various kinds so that standards might be improved, to the benefit of all children.

<u>1) Prayer</u>

Our first task is to pray, always a pre-requisite for action; indeed prayer *is* Christian action of the most valuable and universal kind. Perhaps you have already begun while considering the evidence. We need to be alert to the prompting of the Holy Spirit as we seek his power to bring about change for the better.

PRAY ~~~ for God's guidance, wisdom and discernment;

~~~ that all who share a concern for the well-being of children will become more aware of hidden messages in children's books;

~~~ for enlightenment for those who promote harmful messages;

~~~ that good authors will be successful;

~~~ for discerning people in key positions in education, libraries, and publishing;

~~~ for protection for all concerned, especially the children.

Be willing to be the answer to your prayers!

2) Resolution

Resolve to take more interest in the books read by your children – your own and also your nieces, nephews, grandchildren, your day-school or Sunday school class, young customers in your shop, borrowers in your library. Make a conscious decision to spend time, as much as you can though a little is better than none, acquainting yourself with your children's daily diet of words.

Become involved. Visit the library or bookshop *with* your children. Teach them how to choose books. Be influential in their choices, and so lay the foundations for the development of their own discernment. Your patience will be rewarded.

Offer to help in your school library, or to assist your child's teacher as a reading mum or dad. Acquainting yourself with current trends in this way need take no more than 1-2 hours per week, but will be much appreciated by the staff. If you are restricted by a pre-school child, arrange to share baby-sitting with a friend. Though time is at a premium, it is one of the most precious gifts we can give the next generation.

The greatest burden falls upon teachers, because it is not librarianship but delivery of the curriculum, with all its pressures, which is their primary role. Even so, their work demands responsible handling of unlimited quantities of printed matter. It would be unreasonable to expect them all to have a thorough knowledge of every book in their school. Schools need to acknowledge the urgency of having a strategy to deal with his problem.

It is helpful to draw up a book-buying/borrowing policy and a set of guidelines clearly outlining the school's criteria for selection of reading materials. This should be by consultation between governors and staff, together with the possible participation of some parents. Time spent at this initial stage is time saved later.

The questions I have posed throughout this study may be used as a check-list to guide your own assessments and choices. Use them to check all existing and incoming books. Head-teachers may prefer to summarise them in a simpler, user-friendly format, readily accessible to staff and parents alike. It takes courage to make sweeping changes. The co-operation of a parents' working group sympathetic to the school policy will be invaluable.

Despite their heavy workload, perhaps each member of staff would be willing to read one book per month from the school library. Their views and ratings, weighed against school guidelines, could be noted in a folder or scrapbook available in the staffroom, with recommendations for action.

3) Assessment

Just as parents guide the way their children meet with increasingly adult situations in real life, so there is a need to monitor the pace at which they experience life through the imaginary world of literature. Those responsible for their welfare need to keep one step ahead, foreseeing the dangers and making decisions about the way to proceed.

The motivation by which adults assess young fiction will depend on their particular interest in and responsibility to the child. Parents, with their intimate knowledge of their own offspring, will weigh a story's likely effect on personality and behaviour. Teachers will be largely interested in literary and educational considerations, whilst librarians strive to satisfy consumer demand and at the same time provide a fully comprehensive resource centre. For many authors, booksellers and publishers the major concern would appear to be profit!

First Impressions

When a child selects a book for himself he will almost certainly be attracted by a colourful cover, exciting pictures or the readability of the print. Adults too will want to ensure that this is a story that just *asks* to be read, whether to stimulate little Johnny's interest in reading, or to keep him quiet! A thrifty buyer will, of course, be concerned about practical details – the durability of the binding, the strength of the paper. Both the quality of the publication and a fair price will be high on our list of criteria.

However, as we have discovered, one can rarely rely on first impressions. Adult assessments must delve deeper than these superficial attractions, but much can be learned from even a cursory inspection. Pictures make an immediate impact and on closer examination reveal the general atmosphere. *Elidor's* chaotic line-drawings suggest the blackness of a nightmare. *Fighting Fantasy* books carry symbols of death on most pages. Even picture books may reveal signs of the occult and New Age.

Can we trust promotions?

Useful clues may be gleaned from the dust-jacket or publicity blurb which gives a summary of the contents, often quoting an exciting passage from the text. However, beware of glowing reviews by the "experts" which can be rather ambiguous. A School Library Journal judged *The Witches* to be "Fast moving, well-paced". Is this really any recommendation? What does it tell us about the story? When a media review asserts that an author is without doubt one of the very best writers for children, one is entitled to ask, "By what standard do you measure?"

Others have received awards for their work: *Winnie the Witch* won the Children's Book Award; Carnegie Medal winners include Margaret Mahy, for *The Haunting*, and Susan Cooper for *The Dark is Rising*; Bawden's *Peppermint Pig* won The Guardian Children's Fiction Award in spite of its coarse language. The Federation of Children's Book Groups has named *My Head Teacher is a Vampire* by Pamela Butchart as the overall winner of the Children's Book Award for 2016. Voted for entirely by children, it wins the "Books For Younger Readers" category and is available to view on-line. The opening pages refer to ghosts and contain doubtful messages regarding hauntings. We return to the question: "Is *any* book a child wants to read a good book?"

Children's television often features books and authors. Can we trust its judgement? *Moondial* and *Carrie's War* were dramatised as serials. The writings of Ruth Thomas were highlighted on a Schools programme, persuading me to read *The Secret.* This is the story of a girl and her younger brother left to cope on their own for a week when their mother disappears. Unknown to the children, she has lost her memory as the result of a road accident whilst on an illicit weekend with her boyfriend. I found disturbing messages here about horrid fathers, hypocritical Christians and broken marriages being "bad luck".

Checking Credentials

With further scrutiny of the opening pages, or the title's website, one may discover other works in the same series which throw light on the publisher's policy preferences. Julia MacRae Books have described their Redwing series for 7-11s, and Blackbirds for 10-14s, as presenting many varied viewpoints, of which the Muslim community is just one. Heinemann's Banana Books for 7-9 year-olds were heralded as "bright, funny and brilliantly imaginative… by some of today's top writers", who included, Judy Blume, Douglas Hill, Rose Impey, Joan Aiken and Penelope Lively.

Of course some stories in this series are good and we must bear in mind that many writers have a wide variety of styles and plots, depending on the particular readership they are targeting, but this also applies to those whose books we enjoy. Just because we are impressed by our first encounter with an author's work, we cannot assume subsequent titles will fulfil our expectations. A writer we may have previously considered acceptable will develop his style and pursue new avenues to satisfy the market.

Roderick Hunt, famous for the *Biff, Chip and Kipper* series (Oxford Reading Scheme) has also written *Ghosts, Witches and Things Like That*, a "how to" book for children about the occult with tips for a successful Hallowe'en party. J.H.Brennan, author of *Shiva,* the Ice-Age fantasy, has written *The Aquarian Guide to the New Age* and *The Astral Projection Workbook* for adults. A little more detective work on the internet may provide background information about an author's life and philosophy which causes us to inspect his work more carefully.

Whilst some trade names might ring warning bells, others will be totally misleading. Publicity handouts, distributed to schools, advertising book fairs can give the impression that their materials are associated with education when, in fact, what they teach is not at all beneficial! It is wise to inspect their catalogues before accepting their services.

Assessment of Contents

Having made an initial assessment of a particular volume and judged it worthy of further attention, read its contents with an alert mind, considering the overall thrust of the plot, the intentions of the author, the messages being delivered, the questions posed and the answers given. Especially significant is the attitude of the hero, the character of greatest influence. He is not expected to be a paragon of virtue, for that would not be credible, but one who regrets his mistakes and resolves to make amends. Does he offer hope and inspiration to the reader? Is he a suitable friend?

First, form a general impression. Is the atmosphere confused or one that leads the child on into life at its best? If the story begins with negativity, has the mood changed by the end? What values are held by the characters that will command a child's respect? Be watchful for statements and attitudes which conflict with Biblical truth without being refuted in any way in the text. It is certainly a wise precaution for a teacher to scan the entire contents of a novel before reading it aloud to a class.

Remember that youngsters will take a story at face value. Unless highly intelligent, they will not delve for hidden meanings until they are more mature. Most will not be interested in psychological reasons for the hero's bad behaviour; he will be regarded as a role-model. On the other hand, underlying values and themes will be absorbed by the child's subconscious and form part of a conditioning process at work on his developing adulthood.

Literary Style

Most teachers, and probably parents too, would expect junior fiction to have some literary value, developing the basic English language skills of grammar and spelling, and also enriching the vocabulary. Sadly, nowadays many books are more of a hindrance than a help. You have probably noticed the poor written style of many quotes throughout this book.

Teachers will take a dim view of such expressions as "got to get", used and repeated in *The Little Explorer* by Margaret Joy; "muck about", in *Oi! Get Off Our Train* by Burningham; "didn't do nothing" uttered by the hero of *Tatty Apple*, or "nothink" as *Snakey Boo* would say.

The influx of American material has not helped. One such, *Everyone Else's Parents Said Yes,* continually swings between tenses. There is also confusion over the usage of "lay" or "lie", and the pronouns "them" or "those", "he" or "him". In *The Ghost's Playground*, "him and Mary were always the last ones in".

The tendency for the story to be told in the first person creates its own problems. In an attempt to portray a natural style, Queen's English gives way to colloquialisms: there is the danger of reinforcing bad grammar and the use of slang. The heroine of *Blubber* says, "Me and Tracy are the only ones…" Even in Elizabeth Beresford's *Emily and the Haunted Castle*, which has no ghosts at all and is actually a very good story, Emma says, "Ed and me can swim".

Bernard Ashley's style is very casual: he continually turns clauses into new sentences, e.g. "Which is why she spent…" His first chapter of *I'm Trying to Tell You* is unfortunately in West Indian dialect which renders it an even more disastrous example!

Whereas pupils are usually taught to avoid starting a sentence with "and" or "but", except occasionally for special effect, many authors commit this sin continually, even beginning paragraphs with these conjunctions. In *Master of Fiends*, Hill begins sentences with "And" and "But" as many as seven times per page. Examples may also be found in Aiken's *A Necklace of Raindrops*, recommended in the National Curriculum as assessment material at Key Stage 1. In Marjorie Darke's *Imp*, Gillie buys a calculator – "Took a lot of saving up though. Weeks of pocket money. And I did odd jobs…"

Problem Areas

Having considered our overall impressions of a particular volume, we must now address specific problem areas. I would dispute the assertion that if a story fulfils all other criteria, then one flaw may be overlooked. That is tantamount to burying one's head in the sand and is the loophole through which most books have arrived in our junior libraries. It is their collective influence which is so cunningly potent. We must be prepared to grapple with hard questions, for the spiritual and moral health of young people is at stake.

Difficulties occur when a story majors on an admirable theme, yet harbours undesirable elements as well. *Grange Hill Rebels* delivers a strong warning against drug-taking, yet is careless over attitudes to authority. *Victor's Party* by Townson highlights the difficulties of a loner forced to be more sociable. What a pity she makes brief reference to a graveyard as a "spooky place". Bowkett speaks out powerfully about the horrors of role-playing fantasy in *Gameplayers*, yet his characters blaspheme and convey doubtful views of marriage and the law. Alison Morgan's portrayal of a handicapped boy, in *The Raft*, is admirable, yet one is uneasy with his success won through lies and disobedience. In fact one harmful message skilfully made would outweigh many good messages.

With so many stumbling blocks, one might feel tempted to try to prioritise, but this would be an impossible task, neither should there be any compunction to do so. Does honesty justify violence? Is a swear word more or less offensive than sexual immorality? Is a drunken father a worse influence than a poor image of God? Difficult decisions are called for.

Since all germs cause disease, one should not tolerate any of them. However, just as doctors treat various illnesses by different methods, so with discernment we will choose the most appropriate action to be taken regarding problem books, dealing with each one as an individual case.

As an example, let us imagine we are making an assessment of Elizabeth Beresford's *Rose*, an intriguing mystery in which an old manor provides the setting for a film. On the first page, Rose's divorced mother (A) is reading her stars (B) from the newspaper. The manor is said to be haunted (C), and blond, blue-eyed Rose (D) makes a habit of telling lies (E)! Weighing each point carefully, we discover that:

(A) The issue of single parenthood is ably portrayed, indicating the hardship of marriage breakdown and the rightness of the family set-up.

(B) Horoscopes are mentioned only once with no consequence.

(C) Allegations proved untrue: intruders are human.

(D) Not linked with psychic or super-human ability.

(E) Rose realises the foolishness of telling lies.

Only (B) is an unresolved problem. With adequate discussion in other contexts about the dangers of horoscopes, this book may pass muster for the junior bookshelf.

On the other hand, in the light of reports of juniors taking scrabble letters to school to play ouija, it is likely that assessors will reject *Elidor*, despite its thrilling plot, because of its favourable portrayal of the planchette. In judging the merits of each book it is not enough to say, "This book develops the imagination." The question is, "Having read it, what *images* will *fill* my child's imagination?"

4) To Ban or Not to Ban

Though many would prefer to be told exactly which titles to avoid, others sincerely believe that a published list of banned books would be counter-productive, especially if these volumes are readily available, tempting youngsters to enjoy forbidden fruits. Such a list, whilst being unmanageably long and constantly in need of updating, would allow individuals to shelve their responsibility to be watchful. However, this view has resulted in little being done to tackle the problem.

We can no longer take the easy way out and avoid the issues. For too long, apathy and ignorance have allowed much harm to be done under our very noses. The time has come to make a stand, to speak up like the child who exposed the truth about *The Emperor's New Clothes* (Hans Christian Andersen). Enough is enough! We do not want our children influenced by such material. In order to raise literary standards, we must question what they read.

Most of us exercise a certain degree of self-regulation already with regard to printed matter. For our children, we just need to adjust our focus in the light of current findings. If adults are prepared to make their own assessments of their children's books, based on the principles and guidelines suggested in this survey, and if their findings produce a negative evaluation of a story, then they must seriously consider rejecting it.

Whilst parents have a prerogative to ban unsuitable books from the home, this requires a tactful, sensitive approach bearing in mind the age of the child. It behoves us all to be consistent and give a similar lead with regard to our own reading matter and television programmes! Careful discussion and explanation will be needed with older children, after which, if they choose to rebel it will be a matter for their own conscience. At least they will know the values their parents uphold.

There is no reason why individual schools should not draw up their own list of dubious titles, authors and series, updated when necessary, for in-house use so that all staff may be aware what should be removed from classroom stocks, avoided in the library van, or sent back to booksellers and publishers. This would increase efficiency by reducing the number of books needing detailed scrutiny. The unobtrusive removal of rejected books from a school library will be more expedient than issuing dire warnings.

Though library stocks might fall to rather a low level after radical pruning, this is surely better than shelves being full of harmful material. They can be replenished as and when possible. Poor financing from education authorities may be subsidised by fund-raising projects. Some head-teachers suggest that parents might wish to donate a book to the school, perhaps when their children leave, choosing from a number of recommended titles!

A tried and tested policy is to buy in reference books, but to use the School Library Service for a continually changing supply of fiction. This is a safeguard against wasting money on unsuitable books by mistake and gives an opportunity to express opinions concerning rejects. The system requires constant vigilance and only works well with the co-operation of staff choosing books according to the school guidelines.

Children's public libraries could be far more discriminating about the stock on display. Many hold double standards. Whilst opposing censorship on moral grounds, they boycott Christian writers. Every library should revise its own book-buying policy in the light of current trends, both literary and ethical, and include more Christian books since this is our heritage. They could consider keeping certain titles under cover, only for loan at special request. In the same way, it would be good to see book-shops exercising a responsible attitude for the sake of their reputation.

Of course, it is important to refrain from passing on our rejected books to jumble sales and second-hand book fairs where some other child would be influenced by them. The challenging example of the Ephesians was to burn their occult books without thought for the cost (Acts 19:19)!

5) Discussion

It is so important for parents to develop the habit of talking naturally with their children about any subject without embarrassment. Parents have a God-given mandate to pass on received truths to the next generation "when you sit at home and when you walk along the road, when you lie down and when you get up" (Deut. 6:7). If we do not fulfil these obligations, those who have no knowledge of God will dominate the thinking and behaviour of our young people.

The value of reading aloud to our children, even after they have learned to read well for themselves, cannot be stressed too much. Take turns with them to read alternate pages for extra practice. This gives ample opportunity to discuss issues as they arise in the story. With problem areas of a social or moral nature, this may be the most appropriate type of action to take. With children seated on either side, possibly following the text, be prepared to explain why you have omitted to read the swear-word, or skipped a distasteful passage. Show them how these things are contrary to God's highest will for us.

Until pupils move up to the secondary schools, which can be as late as thirteen-years-old where transfer is from a middle school, parents still have considerable influence over the choices made by their children. They are able to monitor what they buy or borrow. Beyond this age it becomes more difficult; young teens begin to assert their independence. They are vulnerable to greater outside influences: peer pressure, advertising, and numerous teachers with various philosophies. One would hope that by this stage they would have learned at least the rudiments of discernment, according to the values they have been taught at home. As they mature they will need self-motivation to choose carefully for their own moral and spiritual health.

Choose the right moment to ask older children about the novels they are reading and discuss the issues raised. Some subjects could be classed as private rather than vulgar and here sensitivity and tact are needed. Passages like this provide opportunities to introduce intimate matters more easily.

There is also much scope for valuable discussion amongst adults. Share your concern with other parents; raise it as an item at the P.T.A.; alert your church fellowship. Ensure that book-buying relatives are aware of your views before they invest in your family's Christmas presents!

By all means bring your complaints before teachers and librarians, but first make friends with them. Enter into casual exchanges over literary matters and build up a pleasant relationship from which you may pursue your arguments on a better footing, in a controlled and persuasive way. Little progress is made by belligerent confrontation which only forces opponents to defend their corner.

It is well to remember that we have a right to comment and need not feel ashamed to have a Christian viewpoint. To set out with a defensive attitude, appearing prickly from the start, is not conducive to effective communication. Here is an opportunity to use the Christian prophetic gift in a natural way (avoiding "Thus saith the Lord…" at all costs!) to raise awareness of God outside the church walls and to stir people to action.

Responsible teachers can do much to counteract the effects of deceptive messages during class discussions. Great care and wisdom are essential when studying a controversial novel, with special regard to youngsters' feelings and the wishes or their parents. However, librarians must assume that most books will be read alone, with no corrective parallel teaching.

6) How to Complain

Whether we choose to ban any book, or simply discuss and pray through the issues, there are many instances when, for the sake of public awareness and protection of children in general, a spoken or written complaint would seem to be the necessary and appropriate action to take. A few brave parents have dared to protest – lonely voices crying in the wilderness – with varying degrees of success. Those who have shared their concern with a class-teacher have often achieved exemption from a particular book for their *own* children, but this is as far as it goes. Those who have written to libraries have sometimes met with cool rebuttals.

How might we be more effective? No longer can we leave the action to a few brave souls who are regarded as a weird minority with way-out opinions. We must all be willing to speak up and make it plain that we will not be stifled. The strength of our voice lies in numbers, which cannot be easily ignored. Enlist the help of friends; work as groups rather than individuals to highlight widespread concern. Public awareness is heightened when you send one letter but ten would be even better!

By all means quote Scripture, but sparingly, well-placed like a sword to the heart of the matter for greatest effect. Your own translation into everyday language will be adequate. It is not the Biblical prose that holds power but the precepts behind it. Take up the shield of faith and the belt of truth, but resist the temptation to preach a sermon! To effectively disarm your opponent, be firm but gentle, persistent but patient, self-controlled and courteous. Having weighed your criteria against Biblical principles, have confidence and peace of mind.

To whom should we write? To teachers, librarians, booksellers, authors, publishers, newspapers, magazines, clergy, the Association of Christian Teachers, to anyone with influence. Be honest; say what you mean and explain without jargon why certain books are offensive to you. If possible describe their effect on your child. Your feelings and experience of life, and those of your children, *are* valid. You write on behalf of a silent majority, so point out the real dangers to society at large. Make practical, constructive suggestions and specific requests – for a reply, for the removal of a book, or a change in policy.

Letters to Teachers

Write expecting a sympathetic response, avoiding personal attacks. Remember, your child has to face his teacher every day! When pressing for a book to be removed from a reading *scheme*, you may expect to meet some resistance since such a move would cause a gap between the levels of difficulty. Suggest that this might be compensated for by inserting another book at a similar level.

If you are still not satisfied, take the case to the head-teacher, and after that to a school governor, requesting the issue be raised at a governors' meeting. You may be given the chance to attend the meeting and explain your views and the Biblical basis for them. The minutes would be available for parents to read, thus giving excellent publicity to your cause.

Letters to Libraries

There has been some resistance from librarians to letters of complaint, so it is as well to be forewarned of their main lines of defence! Their standard arguments tend to fall into the following five categories: –

1) "Oh but we've always stocked it".

OR "We meet the needs of the total population".

Both imply that no-one else has complained, so you must be the odd one out!

2) The "We are the experts" syndrome – implies parents' ignorance.

"Experienced professional libraries" – means nothing if their values are suspect.

"Much discussion" – is a relative statement and does not specify the nature of their discussion.

3) "This book has fallen into the wrong hands".

OR "Children have freedom of choice"

AND "Children know what they enjoy"

This is a shifting of responsibility on to the children and shows a lack of understanding of the problem.

4) "Well-written, imaginative, unusual," etc. – justifies nothing; a skilfully delivered message is most influential.

5) "This is a well-known, much acclaimed author". – This means: "We don't want to stand out from the crowd."

Aim to explode their ammunition before it is fired. Emphasise their social responsibility. Parents too are experienced with children and give this subject much discussion. Be well-informed and explain the harmful effects of such books on society. Concentrate on fundamental issues widely accepted by Christians such as bad language or the dangers of the occult. More people complain to the television companies about swearing than any other issue, so you have the support of public opinion on this one. Keep your feet on firm ground and avoid personal bees in the bonnet in this arena

Letters to Authors

It is very important to praise and encourage good authors. Contact them through their publishers. As a general rule, assume that writers are motivated by the best of intentions and wish no harm on young readers. If you are worried about tendencies to change their style, point out to them the possible dangers to youngsters. Inform them of other courses of action open to you.

Use clear persuasive arguments, explaining the Christian point of view and also your personal reaction to the authors' work. Challenge them, as skilled writers, to produce exciting books which are not harmful.

Letters to Publishers and Booksellers

Send back books which do not meet your standards and explain why. Books available for sale on-line give space for honest customer reviews on the websites. If booksellers and publishers never receive adverse comments, they may interpret your silence as approval. As with libraries, present a strong case. Challenge their integrity over the matter of profit. Urge a change of policy direction with regard to children's books. Express your desire to find a publisher whom you can trust and support.

Give praise where it is due and request reprints of good literature. My local bookshop manager was delighted when I complimented his display of children's classics. Even Christian publishers, or Christian organisations which recommend lists of books, may not satisfy your personal standards. Open up a dialogue with them, listening to their point of view, but also explaining clearly your objections.

7) Boycotting the Bad

Collectively we have "consumer power". If parents refuse to buy certain books, the withdrawal of their financial support will significantly affect the profit margins of those who exploit our youngsters. Even greater is the power of head teachers whose schools provide a considerable market. In public libraries, data relating to book-loans is stored on computer. Boycotting of certain titles would be automatically recorded. If a book is not being borrowed, it cannot justify its shelf-space.

Drum up support for this action from other parental and educational groups. Form a united front with teachers, librarians and booksellers who share the same concern. Inform those responsible for these books of your intention to act in this way, thus bringing them under pressure to reconsider.

8) Promoting the Good

The other side of this coin is the promotion of good books and the support of their authors and publishers.

A) Be a positive influence on public opinion by organising "Good Book" displays in your school, library, bookshop or church.

B) Consult your local head teacher about starting your own book club for the benefit of the school. There may be cost-cutting deals available.

C) Encourage your church to donate good books to schools and libraries. Explore the help available from charities such as "Speaking Volumes", a scheme which recommends a variety of titles with underlying Christian values.

D) Support your local Christian bookshop and encourage them to "sell themselves" to schools and libraries, perhaps as book agents, or by organising their own book fairs.

E) Create a demand for books with Christian values, at your library and high street book stores. Let them know that here is a market worth pursuing.

F) Write to the Fellowship of Christian Librarians to encourage them and offer support as they seek to influence the choice of stock.

G) Contact other sympathetic organisations, such as the Association of Christian Teachers (A.C.T.), and the Fellowship of Christian Writers, urging them to take action.

H) Offer to speak at schools' Christian Unions to alert students about the conditioning process to which they have been subjected.

I) Work from the inside, by becoming a school governor, library assistant, or P.T.A. member.

J) Write your own books! Work towards redressing the balance. Children need exciting stories which will also inspire them to excellence. There is a scarcity of Christian authors who can write well *and* satisfy the expectations of the modern child.

Conclusion

Youngsters are being exploited in a new way. They are regarded as consumers, both by those who have an eye for financial gain, and by propagandists who are jumping on the bandwagon of junior fiction in order to sell their own particular theories. As the general decline in values has spread throughout society, it has of course affected the literary world.

Most modern children's books are of a secular nature. Far from promoting Christian truth, they range widely, from humanist to pagan standpoints, with many shades between. Young minds are being conditioned to a confusing array of messages. The majority of people considered to be responsible adults may well be oblivious to these dangers. Nonetheless, layers of untruth are being built up in the collective consciousness of the younger generation. The values they absorb will shape their future. By helping our children to understand why certain themes are harmful, we can counteract the deception.

Christianity values childhood. Whereas paganism detests innocence, in Jesus, God himself entered this world as a child, bringing innocence and simple faith. He exhorts us to be like children, to accept his ways and his blessing. The abuse of children aroused passionate emotions in Jesus. He cursed any person or thing that would cause them to sin, foretelling disaster to the world as a result:

"If anyone causes one of these little ones who believe in me to sin, it would be better for him to have a large millstone hung around his neck and to be drowned in the depths of the sea. Woe to the world because of the things that cause people to sin". (Matt.18 : 6-7).

It follows therefore that if we strive to obey the teachings of Christ and bring our children to a knowledge of him, so that they also may avail themselves of Godly wisdom and discernment, we will act in the best interests of all, for the sake of a peaceful and orderly society.

It is clear that Jesus recognised that the children need special protection, being less able to cope with challenges that adults take in their stride. Our aim must be to enable young people to eventually make discerning choices for themselves without too many disasters on the way. Bringing them through to maturity requires loving and sensitive care. We must resist the tide and, with concerted effort, make our protests known so that whatsoever things are true, noble, right, pure, admirable, excellent and praiseworthy may prevail! (Phil. 4 : 8).

No-one having read this book can say, "We did not know!" It is our responsibility as adults to influence our children's choices for good and for blessing, for the sake of their future. We must act now while there is still that choice!

APPENDIX: − ASSESSMENT CHECK LIST

The Christian Ethos

A) Does the book comply or conflict with the Christian ethos?

A1) Is God present, or at least, is there room for him?

    1.1: There may be a god present, but which one?

    1.2: If God is present, is his portrayal Biblically accurate?

    1.3: Is Scripture quoted, or paraphrased, accurately and in context?

A2) Is the scenario one that excludes God? If so how?

    2.1: If God is not present, what values are being promoted?

A3) Does the book convey purpose in life?

    3.1: Is life seen to have meaning, order and pattern?

    3.2: Does the book portray life as pure chance?

A4) What is there beyond life?

    4.1: Is death portrayed as final?

    4.2: What message is given about life after death and the spiritual realm?

    4.3: In whose hand is the power over life and death?

A5) How is the church portrayed?

    5.1: What view is given of clergy and churches?

    5.2: How are Christians portrayed?

Good and Evil – The Cosmic Confrontation

A6) Is the traditional battle between good and evil clear or confused?

    6.1: Are the symbols of dark and light used in the conventional way or reversed?

    6.2: Is evil condemned and good seen to be victorious?

    6.3: Are evil and darkness deemed to be necessary, or even good?

    6.4: Does the book imply there are no absolutes – all is relative?

New Age Influences

A7) Are New Age ideas being infiltrated into young fiction?

    7.1: Is there any reference to mind power, telepathy, E.S.P., etc?

    7.2: Are the heroes influenced by spirit-guides?

    7.3: Is there any reference to self-realisation?

    7.4: Are there signs of paganism or witchcraft?

    7.5: Is there reference to the "old religion"?

    7.6: Does the book preach one-world government and peace?

Christian Truth: Values for Life

B) Is Christian teaching endorsed or contradicted?

B1) Are Christian values upheld?

    1.1: Is bad behaviour presented as entertainment?

B2) Is bad language, blasphemy, swearing, etc., regarded as normal, necessary or excusable?

B3) Are rudeness and vulgarity allowed to go unchallenged, used to attract readership, or used gratuitously?

B4) Does the book portray selfishness, greed, or materialism?

B5) How is deception portrayed?

5.1: Is lying seen to be justified or clever?

5.2: Is dishonesty allowed to go unchallenged?

5.3: Are children encouraged into secretive behaviour which is really deceit?

5.4: Are deceit and craftiness admired, or even rewarded?

5.5: What guidance is given regarding a) respect of property and b) stealing?

B6) What is the motivating factor?

6.1: What attitudes are rewarded?

Christian Truth: Personal Relationships

B7) Does the book make it clear that a stable family unit is the ideal?

7.1: Are parents shown to be loving, wise and a safe refuge?

7.2: Does the father match up to the Christian model of fatherhood?

7.3: Is the mother true to the feminine role?

7.4: How do the siblings relate to one another?

B8) How do fictional children relate to their elders?

    8.1: Do the children respect their parents?

    8.2: Do we see models for right attitudes to older people, e.g. grandparents?

B9) Is the reader given a positive view of authority?

B10) Are children learning how to relate to their peers?

    10.1: Are they being taught to be prejudiced against minorities?

    10.2: What messages are being given regarding boy/girl relationships and sexual morality?

"Isms", Bandwagons, and Propaganda

C) Is the book being used as a medium of propaganda?

C1) Does the book present superstition, folk-lore or personal philosophies as truth?

C2) Does the book contain unsuitable adult messages?

C3) Are the children being exposed to political propaganda?

    3.1: Are children being seduced by campaigns with ulterior motives?

C4) Are children being targeted by social campaigns in an unethical manner?

    4.1: Is the author jumping on the latest bandwagon to ensure credibility?

    4.2: Does the book promote the use of alcohol or drugs of any kind?

C5) Is the promotion of equality in accordance with Christian teaching?

5.1: Is there any sexist bias?

5.2: Is the anti-sexist lobby using propaganda for dubious aims?

5.3: Is any racial prejudice evident?

5.4: Is there stereotyping of lifestyle according to social class?

<u>Horror, Danger and Distress</u>

D) *Does the book portray violence or horror in a manner which is harmful to the child?*

D1) Is there a generally aggressive atmosphere in the author's work?

1.1: Is the aggression or violence portrayed as normal, rather than an intrusion to be resisted?

1.2: Is there a gradual build-up of violence or horror, inducing an expectation which needs to be satisfied?

1.3: Does the book contain gratuitous violence or horror?

1.4: Are there explicit descriptions of violence or horror beyond that of the child's own imagination or ability to cope, such as will affect behaviour?

1.5: Is the book likely to frighten children?

D2) Does the book portray dangerous situations irresponsibly?

D3) Are distressing subjects dealt with sensitively?

Fairy Tale and Fantasy

E) Is fantasy used to widen the imagination in a helpful and inspirational way?

E1) In modern fantasy, do acceptable values still hold?

    1.1: Does symbolism lead the reader into spiritual truth, or confusion?

    1.2: Does fantasy clarify reality − or is it gratuitous escapism?

E2) Does our choice of books include adequate variety?

Witches, Ghosts and the Occult

F) Is there a harmful pre-occupation with occult themes?

F1) Does the story stimulate the child's interest by concentrating on the occult for its own sake?

    1.1: Is the reader encouraged to have an unhealthy interest in spirits of the dead?

F2) Is the reader led to empathise or collaborate with those involved in the occult?

    2.1: Is the reader led to empathise with witches and wizards, or admire their power?

    2.11: Is the witch portrayed as harmless, or friendly?

    2.12: Is there an emphasis on the normality of witchcraft?

    2.13: Are witches portrayed as respected members of society?

    2.14: Are witches portrayed as helpful people, perhaps healers?

2.15: Are witches given an attractive, exciting image?

F3) What kind of magic do we find in this story?

3.1: Are there explicit descriptions of occult paraphernalia, encouraging a child to experiment?

3.2: Is there explicit information about spells, charms and ritual?

F4) Is the overall treatment of the theme a true and balanced representation of occultism?

4.1: Is the book likely to worry or frighten a reader?

4.2: Does the book, series or collection stimulate a child's expectancy of occult activity or exploit its entertainment value?

Humour – What Are Our Children Laughing At?

G) *Are children being taught to laugh inappropriately?*

G1) Are children being taught to enjoy dark humour?

1.1: Are children being taught that sin is to be laughed at?

1.2: Are children being encouraged to laugh at indecency and vulgarity?

1.3: Are children being taught to laugh disrespectfully?

1.4: Are children learning to laugh cruelly at misfortune?

1.5: Are children being encouraged to laugh at the macabre and grotesque?

G2) Are children expected to laugh senselessly?

G3) Does the book contain adult humour?

Action Stations!

H) What Action Can Be Taken?

35093261R00147

Printed in Great Britain
by Amazon